YOUNG STUDENTS

Learning Library

VOLUME 17

Poultry–Rococo Art

WEEKLY READER BOOKS

MIDDLETOWN · CONNECTICUT

PHOTO CREDITS

AMERICAN MUSEUM OF PHOTOGRAPHY page 2094(bottom left); AMERICAN RED CROSS page 2073(center right); AUSTRIAN INFORMATION SERVICE page 2024(bottom right); AUSTRIAN RAILWAY page 2054(bottom center); BBC page 2052(top left); BTA page 2101(bottom center); BBC HULTON PICTURE LIBRARY page 1999(top right); 2032(bottom left); 2035(center right); 2062(top left); 2077(top right); 2095(top right & bottom left); 2103(top right); BIRTIN & CIE page 2059(bottom left); JEAN F. BLASHFIELD page 2031(bottom right); BOEING page 2043(top right); BRITISH MUSEUM(NATURAL HISTORY) page 2087(bottom right); BRITISH RAIL page 2056(center left); BULLOZ page 2114(top left); CANADA HOUSE page 2053(bottom left); J. ALLAN CASH page 2059(bottom right); 2101(top right); MICHAEL CHINERY page 2077(bottom center); BRUCE COLEMAN LIMITED page 2040(bottom left); DAVE COLLINS page 2081(top right); CROSFIELD ELECTRONICS LIMITED page 2003(bottom right); ARMANDO CURCIO EDITORE SPA page 1993(top right); 1998(top left); 2000(top & center left); 2007(bottom right); 2008(both pics); 2012(top left); 2018(top left); 2028(top left); 2042(top left & bottom right); 2054(top left); 2061(top right); 2062(center left); 2067(bottom left); 2068(top left); 2072(top right); 2075(top right); 2080(top left); 2083(bottom right); 2084(top left & top right); 2085(both pics); 2086(top left and bottom); 2087(top left); 2090(top left); 2095(bottom right); 2097(bottom right); 2100(top left); 2101(bottom right); 2102(both pics); 2105(top left); 2106(bottom left); 2113(top right); C.O.I. page 2040(bottom right); EMI page 2072(bottom pics); EDINBURGH UNIVERSITY LIBRARY page 2096(top left); DOROTHY M. EVANS page 2104(bottom left); EPA/PICTORIAL PARADE page 2051(bottom right); GEOLOGICAL MUSEUM page 2108(top left); GERMAN RAILWAYS page 2055(top left); GIRAUDON page 2075(bottom right); SONIA HALLIDAY page 2011(top right); 2080(bottom center); ROBERT HARDING PICTURE LIBRARY page 2010(bottom left); RUSSELL F. HOGELAND page 2021(bottom right); MICHAEL HOLFORD page 2084(bottom left); IMITOR page 2016(bottom right); INDIA HIGH COMMISSION page 2000(top right); KOBAL COLLECTION page 2030(left); LIBRARY OF CONGRESS page 2069(top right); 2070(top left); MANSELL COLLECTION page 2016(top left); 2082(top left); MARCONI page 2043(bottom right); MAURITSHUIS, THE HAGUE page 2082(bottom left); PAT MORRIS page 2040(top left); NASA page 2044(top right); 2107(bottom right); 2110(bottom right); NHPA page 1992(bottom left); 2065(bottom right); NATIONAL GALLERY OF ART, WASHINGTON, D.C. page 2068(bottom left); 2083(top right); 2113(center right); NATIONAL TRUST page 2114(bottom right); NATIONAL SCIENCE PHOTOS page 2091(top right); NATURE PHOTOGRAPHERS page 2097(top right); OAK RIDGE NATIONAL LABORATORY page 2049(bottom left); D. OLIVER page 2048(top left); PARAMOUNT PICTURES page 2058(top right); PENNSYLVANIA RAILROAD page 2058(bottom left); PHOTRI page 2001(center left); 2005(top right); 2020(top left); 2042(bottom left); 2052(bottom left); 2099(top right); PICTUREPOINT page 2010(top right); 2013(top right); 2022(top left); DAVID REFERN page 2071(top right); RENAULT page 2107(bottom left); RHODE ISLAND DEVELOPMENT COUNCIL page 2014(top left); MAX PLANCK INSTITUTE FOR RADIO ASTRONOMY page 2050(top left); ROYAL ASTRONOMICAL SOCIETY page 2051(top right); SATOUR page 2090(bottom); SCALA page 2015(bottom right); SEABOARD SYSTEM RAILROAD page 2057(top left); SNCF page 2053(bottom right); SONY page 2047(top right); SPECTRUM COLOUR LIBRARY page 1992(top right); 1994(top right); 2074(bottom left); 2076(top left); TEXAS HIGHWAY DEPT. page 2104(top left); JOHN TOPHAM PICTURE LIBRARY page 2022(bottom right); TRANS-WORLD AIRLINES page 2079(bottom right); USDA PHOTO page 2029(top right); ULLSTEIN page 2010(top left); UNITED KINGDOM ATOMIC ENERGY AUTHORITY page 2049(top right); UNIVERSITY OF NOTRE DAME page 2112(top left); VISHNIAC LABORATORY PHOTO page 2017(top right); ZEFA page 1991(both pics); 2001(top right & bottom left); 2019(both pics); 2023(top); 2024(top left); 2026(bottom left); 2031(top right); 2034(top left); 2037(bottom left); 2038(top left); 2055(top right); 2057(top right); 2060(bottom right); 2061(bottom right); 2089(top left); 2092(top left); 2093(top right); 2094(top left); 2096(bottom left); 2098(top right); 2100(bottom left); 2103(bottom right); 2109(top right); 2112(bottom right).

Young Students Learning Library is a trademark of Field Publications.

Copyright © 1990, 1989, 1988, 1982, 1977 Field Publications; 1974, 1972 by Funk & Wagnalls, Inc. & Field Publications.

ISBN 0-8374-6047-6

CONTENTS

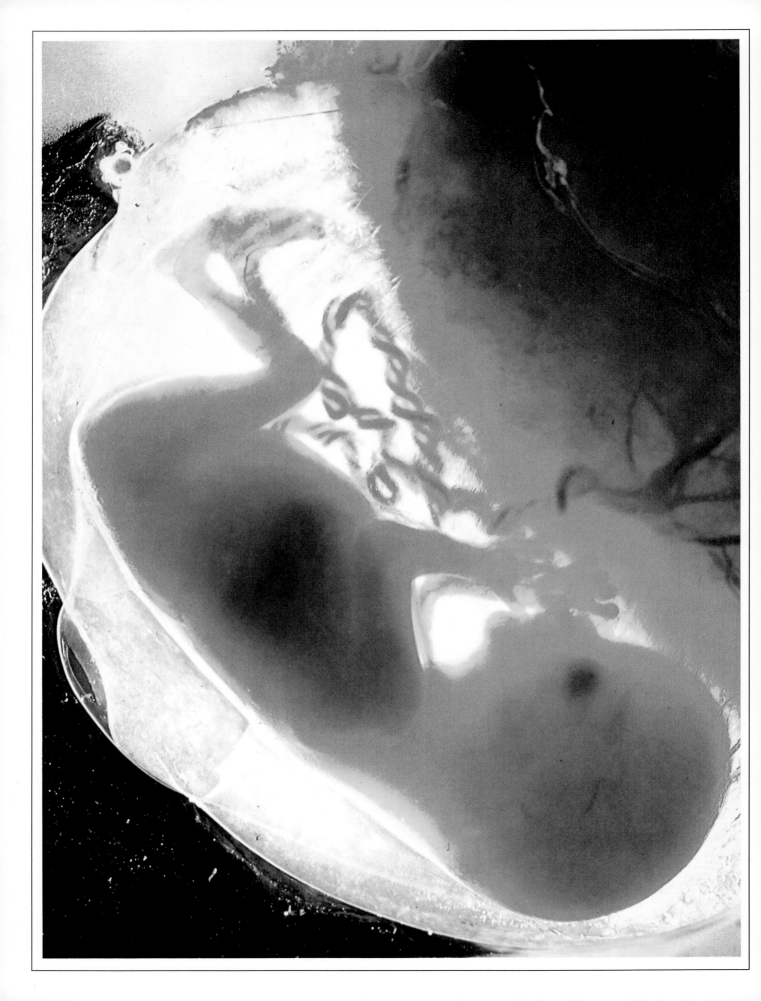

POULTRY Birds raised for their meat and eggs are called poultry. Chickens, ducks, turkeys, geese, guinea fowl, pheasants, and pigeons can all be poultry birds.

In the United States, about 95 percent of all poultry are chickens. A large industry produces chickens and eggs for market. Only a few chicken farms go through all the steps of raising chickens from eggs, selling the eggs laid by these chickens, and also selling chickens for meat. Most large chicken farms specialize in one of the steps that produce eggs and chickens.

All chickens are descended from a type of pheasant still living in the jungles of India. Careful breeding has produced two different kinds of chickens—chickens that are good for meat and chickens that are good for eggs. Meat chickens should grow fat quickly on a small amount of food. The white Plymouth Rock is the most popular meat chicken. Egg-laying chickens should lay a lot of eggs fast and not eat very much or sit very much. White leghorns are the best egg-laying chickens.

Breeders either hatch their own eggs or send them to commercial hatcheries. The eggs are hatched in an *incubator*. An incubator is a heated cabinet that supplies the warmth a mother hen usually supplies for hatching eggs. A large incubator can hold 100,000 eggs. The chicks hatch in about 21 days.

Chicks bred for their meat are called *broiler* chicks. They are bought by broiler growers and put in growing houses. The chicks are *brooded*, or kept warm, for the first four to six weeks. Then the heat is turned down. They are fed a rich mash of corn, meat, fish, vitamins, and minerals. In eight

◄ *The miracle of life—a human fetus inside the womb. At the right is the* placenta, *through which the baby gets vital nourishment from its mother.* (See REPRODUCTION.)

to nine weeks, they weigh 3 to 4 pounds (1.4 to 1.8 kg). They are then sold as *broilers* or *fryers*. Older, heavier, tougher chickens are sold as *roasters*, *stewing* chickens, or just plain *fowl*. An unsexed male chicken is called a *capon*.

The female egg-laying chicks, called *pullets*, are sold to egg farmers. The male chicks of egg-laying breeds are usually killed. The pullets are brooded and grown for five months, and then they are put to work laying eggs. On a small farm, a hen might lay eight to ten eggs in a nest and spend three weeks hatching them. But on a large modern egg farm, the eggs are taken away as soon as they are laid, and the hen just keeps laying. On such a farm, a good white leghorn pullet can lay 250 to 300 eggs a year. After 12 to 15 months, pullets are usually killed and sold as stewing chickens, and the egg farmer buys a new flock of pullets.

Four of every 100 poultry fowl are turkeys. Most American families think of eating turkeys at Thanksgiving and at Christmas, but turkeys can be bought at markets all during the year. The markets are supplied by a turkey-raising industry. Until about 30 years ago, the average turkey weighed between 16 and 24 pounds (7.3 and 11 kg). Now farmers and scientists have succeeded in breeding

▲ *This young girl is feeding her free-range chickens—so called because they are free to roam around the farm and are not cooped up like battery chickens.*

▼ *Battery hens produce eggs on a "production line." The eggs roll forward into a trough from which they can be collected.*

We think of chickens as birds that don't fly. This is not really so. It is possible for a chicken to fly for more than 200 feet (60 m).

smaller turkeys, too. The males weigh about 15 pounds (7 kg) and the females about 8 pounds (3.5 kg). This size turkey is popular with small families for Sunday dinner. There is no turkey egg industry.

Not quite two of every 100 poultry fowl are ducks, and almost one in 100 is a goose. Ducks and geese are raised for meat and for feathers. The *down* feathers of these two birds are especially soft and are used to stuff the best pillows and skiers' down jackets. Ducks about eight weeks old are called *ducklings*. They weigh 5 or 6 pounds (2.5 or 3 kg) and are sold for meat. Geese are sold for eating when they are ten weeks old and weigh about 15 pounds (7 kg). Although duck and goose eggs are good to eat, no special industry produces these eggs for market. One kind of duck can lay as many as 360 eggs a year.

In the United States, there are guinea fowl farms in the Midwest and the South. A grown guinea fowl weighs 3 to 3½ pounds (1.4 to 1.6 kg). The pearl (or white) and the lavender guinea fowl are raised as poultry. The pearl has white-dotted, purplish-gray feathers. Guinea fowl are eaten mostly in restaurants.

Pheasants are wild birds, but a few are raised as poultry. Pheasants ready

▲ *A cock turkey struts and fans out its feathers in an impressive display.*

for market weigh about 5 pounds (2.5 kg) each. They, too, are usually sold to restaurants.

When your great-grandparents wanted to eat a chicken, they may have had to pluck it themselves, or they may have bought a live bird and killed it themselves. Then they had the messy job of cleaning it. Today, most chicken and most other poultry is sold cleaned and packaged. And if your parents don't want to buy a whole bird, they can buy the parts instead—wings, breasts, or legs.

ALSO READ: EGG, GAME BIRDS, INCUBATOR, MEAT.

POWER Your parents have a powerful car, but the parents of a friend of yours may have one that is more powerful. One car can go much faster than the other, and it can accelerate (speed up) much more swiftly. But what does the word "powerful" really mean?

To understand the idea of power we have first to understand the idea of work. When scientists use the word "work," they do not mean the type of work you have to do at school.

Imagine two machines that can push heavy weights. If one machine pushes a weight twice as heavy as the

▼ *A handsome male pheasant, with the hen in the background. Like many birds, the male pheasant has striking and colorful plumage that he shows off to attract a mate.*

other does, we say that the machine is doing twice as much work. Likewise, if one machine can push the same weight as the other, but twice as far, we say it is doing twice as much work. To a scientist, the word "work" therefore means the *force* produced by the machine multiplied by the *distance* over which that force works.

But some machines are able to do a lot more work in a given time than others. If the two machines had to push the same weight the same distance, one might be able to do it twice as fast as the other. We say that this machine is twice as *powerful* as the other.

So, when people say that they have a powerful automobile, what they really mean is that the automobile has an engine that can do a lot of work very quickly.

ALSO READ: FORCE.

POWHATAN (about 1550–1618) Powhatan was a wise and powerful Indian chief. He ruled the Powhatan Confederacy, a group of Algonkian-speaking tribes numbering about 9,000 Indians. These Indians lived in villages along the coast of Virginia, where the English made their first permanent settlement in America.

Powhatan's real name was Wahunsonacock. But the English colonists called him "Powhatan" after the name of his favorite village. Powhatan was friendly to the settlers and traded with them.

The people in England who had sent the settlers to Virginia wanted to make a profit on the money they had invested. They demanded that the colonists grow more tobacco. The colonists needed more land, so they began taking Indian land. Naturally, Powhatan and his warriors fought to keep their land.

When Powhatan's daughter, Pocahontas, married a colonist named John Rolfe in 1614, the chief made

peace with the English. But he died four years later, and his brother, Opechancanough, attacked the colonists at Jamestown. Finally, in 1644, the Powhatan Confederacy was defeated. The tribes gradually died out.

ALSO READ: ALGONKIAN; AMERICAN HISTORY; INDIANS, AMERICAN; JAMESTOWN; POCAHONTAS.

PRAIRIE When pioneers headed West in the 1800's, they took their covered wagons over mountains, across rivers, and through forests. Imagine their surprise when they came to a place where there were no mountains, no rivers, no trees—only tall grass waving in the breeze, as far as they could see! The pioneers had reached the prairies.

"Prairie" is a French word, meaning "meadow." A prairie is simply a broad, grassy plain, found in temperate regions. In Argentina this kind of grassland is called the *pampas*. In the Soviet Union, a similar level stretch of

▶ *Prairie soils have three distinct layers, called* horizons. *The A horizon lies beneath the plant cover and contains grains of rock and organic material. The B horizon contains material dissolved from the A horizon. The C horizon is weathered and contains broken-down material from the bedrock below it.*

▲ *According to a legend, Powhatan's daughter Pocahontas saved the life of Captain John Smith, the Jamestown leader. In this picture, Powhatan looks on angrily as Pocahontas stops the upraised tomahawk of one of his braves.*

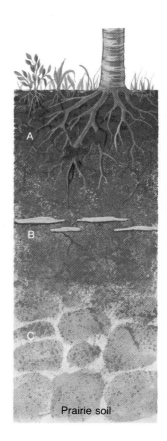

Prairie soil

PRAIRIE DOG

► *Farmland covers what was once prairie grassland in the Midwest.*

The prairie dog builds its home by digging straight down into the earth to a depth that may be as much as 14 feet (4 m). In Arizona, more than 7,000 of these holes have been found in one square mile (2.5 sq. km).

land at a higher elevation is called the *steppes*. In South Africa, the high prairie region is called the *veld* or *veldt*. Large stretches of prairie are also found in Hungary, Romania, Brazil, Uruguay, Canada, and the United States. Prairies in the United States spread across Illinois, Iowa, Oklahoma, Texas, Nebraska, Kansas, North and South Dakota, and parts of other states. Alberta, Saskatchewan, and Manitoba are known as the "Prairie Provinces" in Canada.

Little rain falls on the North American prairie regions. Summers are hot and dry. Few trees grow on the land, but the landscape is broken up by scattered, low hills and riverbeds. Prairie grass is coarse and grows from 2 to 6 feet (60 cm to 2 m) high or even taller. There are many different kinds of prairie grass, including big and little bluestem, wild rye, switch grass, June grass, needlegrass, and slough grass. Prairie grass is rooted in thick, rich soil. A few flowering plants and herbs are usually mixed in with the grass.

Spiders, ants, wasps, beetles, and other insects live among the grasses. Some birds living in the grasslands are hawks, larks, sparrows, prairie chickens, and pheasants. Snakes and toads are common. Prairie dogs, jackrabbits, kangaroo rats, and squirrels live in regions where the grass has been worn down by cattle. Buffalo (bison) once grazed on American

prairies, but most of them were killed by hunters.

The pioneers who settled on the big prairies of the Midwest faced many difficulties. They could not break through the dense sod of the prairies easily with their wooden and iron plows. But in 1837, a blacksmith named John Deere invented the steel plow that cut sharply through the tough soil. Few trees grew on the prairies, so pioneers (called "sodbusters") made huts out of chunks of sod. Then railroads came to the prairie region, and settlers were able to send crops to market and get lumber and other supplies. Today, grain-growing farms and many cattle ranches are spread across the prairies.

ALSO READ: BISON, GRASS, GREAT PLAINS, PRAIRIE DOG, WESTWARD MOVEMENT.

PRAIRIE DOG The prairie dog received its name because it makes a noise similar to a dog's bark. Prairie dogs, also called ground squirrels, are related to both squirrels and marmots.

The prairie dog measures about 14 inches (35 cm) in length, including a bushy tail about 3 inches (8 cm) long. The animal is reddish brown with patches of gray and white. The female prairie dog usually produces four young in a litter. Prairie dogs feed on the vegetation available on dry prairie land.

The prairie dog lives in large underground burrows in the western United States. These burrows, about 10 feet (3 m) under the ground, have so many tunnels that people call the burrows "towns." Hundreds of prairie dog families live in these towns. A rim of earth around the entrance to the burrow prevents it from flooding. A prairie dog usually stands guard at each entrance to the town. If it sees an enemy, it makes a loud barking noise and everyone runs for home.

Before farmers and cattle ranchers came west, the number of prairie dogs was kept down by their natural enemies, such as weasels, wolves, snakes, and hawks. But when the settlers came, they chased away or killed most of these enemies. As a result, the number of prairie dogs grew larger and larger. In some parts of Texas, the towns extended for hundreds of miles underground. This land could not be used because of the tunnels, so farmers killed many of the prairie dogs. The few towns that re-

main are mostly in parts where wildlife is protected.

ALSO READ: MAMMAL, RODENT, SQUIRREL.

PRAYER A prayer is a way of communicating with God. Prayer is practiced differently by people of different religious faiths. It is a form of devotion through which a person can give thanks, ask for help, confess sin, or otherwise approach God. Prayers are often said with the head bowed.

Many Roman Catholics pray with the help of a *rosary*, a circle of 50 small beads made of wood, stone, or metal. From them hangs a *crucifix* (cross) with two large beads and three small ones. On the large beads is said the Lord's Prayer, a special prayer said by many Christians.

ALSO READ: RELIGION. *See also names of individual religions.*

▼ *Prairie dogs live in large communities called towns, each of which is divided into smaller units called coteries. There are perhaps half a dozen adult animals in each coterie, and they and their youngsters form a close "family." They groom each other and play with one another, and at least one animal always seems to be on the lookout for danger.*

PRECIPITATION see WATER, WATER CYCLE.

PREDATOR see CARNIVORE, FOOD WEB.

PREGNANCY see REPRODUCTION.

▼ *Scientists divide the history of life on Earth into eras, which are further divided into periods. The earliest forms of life appeared about 600 million years ago.*

Recent time

Mammals, man-apes appear

CENOZOIC ERA

65 million years ago

Extinction of dinosaurs

MESOZOIC ERA

1st primitive mammals

?25 million years ago

1st reptiles

PALEOZOIC ERA

1st amphibians

1st land plants

1st armored fish

600 million years ago

PREHISTORY About 5,000 years ago someone invented writing, and so history began. People could write about the things that happened, and centuries later other people could read what had been written. But human beings existed for several million years before writing was invented, and the Earth was formed several billion years before that. *Prehistory* is the word we use to describe the time before writing was invented.

The study of prehistory is carried out by scientists of several different types. *Cosmologists* are interested in events so far in the past that they happened even before the Earth existed. They try to work out what happened when the universe sprang into existence. *Historical geologists* study rocks to find out what our planet was like millions of years ago. *Paleontologists* study fossils to see what animals and plants were like during prehistory. And *archeologists* look at the remains of prehistoric human beings—their paintings, their bones, and even their garbage heaps—to find out what our distant ancestors were like.

ALSO READ: ANCIENT CIVILIZATIONS, ARCHEOLOGY, DINOSAUR, FOSSIL, PLANTS OF THE PAST, UNIVERSE.

PREPOSITION see PARTS OF SPEECH.

PRESIDENCY The President of the United States, often called the Chief Executive, is the head of the Federal Government. The President is elected for a four-year term and can serve no more than two terms. A candidate for the Presidency must be a native-born citizen who is at least 35 years old and has lived in the United States for 14 years before running for office.

Article Two of the U.S. Constitution defines many of the President's

THE PRESIDENTS OF THE UNITED STATES AND THEIR VICE-PRESIDENTS

President	Party	Served	Vice-President	Served
1. **George Washington** (1732–1799)	Federalist	1789–1797	John Adams	1789–1797
2. **John Adams** (1735–1826)	Federalist	1797–1801	Thomas Jefferson	1797–1801
3. **Thomas Jefferson** (1743–1826)	Democratic-Republican	1801–1809	Aaron Burr George Clinton	1801–1805 1805–1809
4. **James Madison** (1751–1836)	Democratic-Republican	1809–1817	George Clinton Elbridge Gerry	1809–1812 1813–1814
5. **James Monroe** (1758–1831)	Democratic-Republican	1817–1825	Daniel D. Tompkins	1817–1825
6. **John Quincy Adams** (1767–1848)	Democratic-Republican	1825–1829	John C. Calhoun	1825–1829
7. **Andrew Jackson** (1767–1845)	Democrat	1829–1837	John C. Calhoun Martin Van Buren	1829–1832 1833–1837
8. **Martin Van Buren** (1782–1862)	Democrat	1837–1841	Richard M. Johnson	1837–1841
9. **William H. Harrison** (1773–1841)	Whig	1841	John Tyler	1841
10. **John Tyler** (1790–1862)	Whig	1841–1845		
11. **James K. Polk** (1795–1849)	Democrat	1845–1849	George M. Dallas	1845–1849
12. **Zachary Taylor** (1784–1850)	Whig	1849–1850	Millard Fillmore	1849–1850
13. **Millard Fillmore** (1800–1874)	Whig	1850–1853		
14. **Franklin Pierce** (1804–1869)	Democrat	1853–1857	William R. King	1853
15. **James Buchanan** (1791–1868)	Democrat	1857–1861	John C. Breckinridge	1857–1861
16. **Abraham Lincoln** (1809–1865)	Republican	1861–1865	Hannibal Hamlin Andrew Johnson	1861–1865 1865
17. **Andrew Johnson** (1808–1875)	National Union	1865–1869		
18. **Ulysses S. Grant** (1822–1885)	Republican	1869–1877	Schuyler Colfax Henry Wilson	1869–1873 1873–1875
19. **Rutherford B. Hayes** (1822–1893)	Republican	1877–1881	William A. Wheeler	1877–1881
20. **James A. Garfield** (1831–1881)	Republican	1881	Chester A. Arthur	1881
21. **Chester A. Arthur** (1830–1886)	Republican	1881–1885		
22. **Grover Cleveland** (1837–1908)	Democrat	1885–1889	Thomas A. Hendricks	1885
23. **Benjamin Harrison** (1833–1901)	Republican	1889–1893	Levi P. Morton	1889–1893
24. **Grover Cleveland** (1837–1908)	Democrat	1893–1897	Adlai E. Stevenson	1893–1897
25. **William McKinley** (1843–1901)	Republican	1897–1901	Garret A. Hobart Theodore Roosevelt	1897–1899 1901
26. **Theodore Roosevelt** (1858–1919)	Republican	1901–1909	Charles W. Fairbanks	1905–1909
27. **William H. Taft** (1857–1930)	Republican	1909–1913	James S. Sherman	1909–1912
28. **Woodrow Wilson** (1856–1924)	Democrat	1913–1921	Thomas R. Marshall	1913–1921
29. **Warren G. Harding** (1865–1923)	Republican	1921–1923	Calvin Coolidge	1921–1923
30. **Calvin Coolidge** (1872–1933)	Republican	1923–1929	Charles G. Dawes	1925–1929
31. **Herbert C. Hoover** (1874–1964)	Republican	1929–1933	Charles Curtis	1929–1933
32. **Franklin D. Roosevelt** (1882–1945)	Democrat	1933–1945	John N. Garner Henry A. Wallace Harry S. Truman	1933–1941 1941–1945 1945
33. **Harry S. Truman** (1884–1972)	Democrat	1945–1953	Alben W. Barkley	1949–1953
34. **Dwight D. Eisenhower** (1890–1969)	Republican	1953–1961	Richard M. Nixon	1953–1961
35. **John F. Kennedy** (1917–1963)	Democrat	1961–1963	Lyndon B. Johnson	1961–1963
36. **Lyndon B. Johnson** (1908–1973)	Democrat	1963–1969	Hubert H. Humphrey	1965–1969
37. **Richard M. Nixon** (1913–	Republican	1969–1974	Spiro T. Agnew Gerald R. Ford	1969–1973 1973–1974
38. **Gerald R. Ford** (1913–	Republican	1974–1977	Nelson A. Rockefeller	1974–1977
39. **James E. Carter** (1924–	Democrat	1977–1981	Walter F. Mondale	1977–1981
40. **Ronald W. Reagan** (1911–	Republican	1981–1989	George Bush	1981–1989
41. **George H. Bush** (1924–	Republican	1989–	James Danforth Quayle	1989–

▲ *The inauguration of President James K. Polk took place at the Capitol in March 1845. In the Presidential tradition, Polk swore on the Bible to uphold the Constitution of the United States.*

▲ *The flag of the President of the United States.*

President Andrew Jackson had a group of personal friends and advisers who were called the "Kitchen Cabinet" because they were an unofficial, informal kind of cabinet. Nearly every President since then has had unofficial advisers as well as an official cabinet.

powers. The Constitution separates governmental powers into three areas—legislative, executive, and judicial. The executive branch, headed by the President, has the job of enforcing laws made by the legislative branch, Congress. The Constitution also gives the President the duties of commanding the armed forces, making treaties with foreign nations, and appointing government officials. The President can also pardon (release from prison) people who have been convicted of crimes, except for government officials who have been impeached, and can also grant *reprieves*, or postponements of punishment. The President plans programs and policies with the executive department heads—the Cabinet—and makes a yearly report to Congress on the state of the union. The President can veto (overrule) legislation passed by Congress.

The Presidency has assumed more power through the years as the problems of daily government of the country have increased. Executive orders issued by the President have the force of law. The President has a great deal of influence on the country's economy through powers given by Congress. The President regulates money loaned by banks and interest charged on loans through the Federal Reserve System, and also regulates interstate

commerce (buying and selling) through the Interstate Commerce Commission. The President presents the yearly national budget to Congress. The President is also in charge of U.S. relations with other countries and can make agreements with other countries that are as binding as treaties (which must have the approval of the Senate).

The power to appoint federal officials and remove them from office also gives the President a great deal of power. Some of the most important appointments are those the President makes to the U.S. Supreme Court. These justices often serve for many years after the President has left office. According to the Constitution, the Senate must approve the President's appointments, but in practice, the Senate considers only high-ranking officials. Appointment to governmental office is the most important way in which a President can repay those who have worked in the campaign. The President can also remove officials from office.

The size of the executive branch can give you a good idea of the power and responsibilities of the Presidency. Under the direction of the President are the thirteen executive departments (each employing a large number of people) and many independent agencies, which are often as large as the departments. The executive branch employs most civil service employees, over two million people. Each President also organizes a group of assistants, called the Executive Office, who work in the White House and other buildings.

The Constitution provides for orderly succession to the Presidency. The Twenty-fifth Amendment, adopted in 1967, states that if a President dies or resigns before the term of office ends, the Vice-President becomes President. The President appoints a new Vice-President, with the approval of Congress, should such a vacancy arise.

ALSO READ: CABINET, UNITED STATES; CONGRESS, UNITED STATES; CONSTITUTION, UNITED STATES; IMPEACHMENT; LEGISLATURE; UNITED STATES GOVERNMENT; VICE-PRESIDENT.

PRESLEY, ELVIS (1935–1977)

Who was the first "king" of rock 'n' roll? Most people would answer: Elvis Presley. Elvis Aaron Presley was a star of pop music. His name and songs were known all over the world from the moment he burst onto the scene in 1956.

Elvis Presley was born in Tupelo, Mississippi, on January 8, 1935. He made his first record while working as a truck driver singing country and western music. He was also influenced by black rhythm and blues singers and brought black music to the notice of many people who had never listened to it before.

In 1956 Presley had his first hit: "Heartbreak Hotel." He went on to an amazing career as an entertainer, making hit records that sold millions of copies, and becoming an international idol to millions of fans. He also made a number of films, such as *Love Me Tender* and *Jailhouse Rock*.

Presley was admired and imitated by numerous other pop performers. Fans all over the world mourned his death, at the age of 42, in 1977 in Memphis, Tennessee, where his career had begun.

PRESSURE

Imagine blowing up a balloon. As you blow more air into the balloon, it gets bigger and bigger. If you blow in too much air, the balloon bursts. The pressure of the air becomes too great, and the rubber breaks.

What is pressure? Scientists say that it is force per unit area acting on a surface. This is hard to understand. But imagine you have blown up the balloon and now touch it with a pin. You don't have to push the pin very hard to burst the balloon. But you would have to use quite a lot of force to burst the balloon by squeezing it between your hands. This is because you hands have a far bigger area than the point of the pin. The bigger the area of whatever you press against the balloon, the more force you need to use to burst it.

But why does a balloon get bigger as you blow more air into it? You are making the pressure of the air inside the balloon greater than the pressure of the air outside it. There are many more air molecules inside the balloon than there would be in a similar volume of "normal" air. The molecules are moving around very rapidly, and lots of them hit the inside of the balloon every second—far more than are hitting it from the outside every second.

If you heat the air molecules inside the balloon, they travel even faster, and so the balloon gets bigger. Put a balloon in a hot bath, and see how it has changed when you pull it out of the hot water. But it will soon go back to its old size as the air inside it cools.

ALSO READ: AREA, ATMOSPHERE, FORCE.

PRIESTLEY, JOSEPH (1733–1804)

Joseph Priestley was a British clergyman who is remembered for his chemical experiments. Both he and a Swedish scientist, Karl Wilhelm Scheele, are credited with the discovery of oxygen.

Priestley was born at Fieldhead, England. He studied for the Presbyterian ministry and then served as minister in several churches. Priestley was interested in science. He once heard Benjamin Franklin lecture in London on electricity, and he became very interested in the subject. With Franklin's encouragement, Priestley published *The History and Present State of Electricity* in 1767. Priestley is credited with the discovery of *hydro-*

▲ *Elvis Presley, the "king" of rock 'n' roll.*

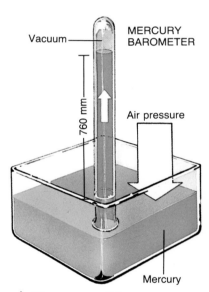

MERCURY BAROMETER

Vacuum

760 mm

Air pressure

Mercury

▲ *The pressure of the atmosphere can be measured with a mercury barometer. The pressure of the air forces the mercury to a certain height in a tube with a vacuum at the top. The height to which it rises depends on the air pressure, which can be measured in millimeters of mercury. Normal atmospheric pressure equals 760 mm of mercury.*

▲ *Joseph Priestley, English scientist.*

Joseph Priestley accidentally discovered that carbon dioxide dissolved in water has a pleasant, tart taste. Today this solution is called soda water.

▲ *Anthony Eden (left), prime minister of Great Britain from April 1955 until January 1957, confers with Russian premier Nikita Khrushchev.*

chloric acid, nitrous oxide (laughing gas), and *sulfur dioxide*. He made his most important discovery in 1774. He heated the compound *mercuric oxide* and obtained a gas. This gas later became known as oxygen.

Priestley continued his work as a minister, becoming a Unitarian. He wrote a number of books on social and religious subjects. Because of his sympathy with the French Revolution, a mob in Birmingham, England, burned Priestley's house and destroyed his books and scientific instruments. Priestley left England and went to the United States in 1791. He lived the rest of his life in Northumberland, Pennsylvania.

ALSO READ: CHEMISTRY; ELEMENT; FRANKLIN, BENJAMIN; OXYGEN.

PRIMATE see APE, HUMAN BEING.

PRIME MINISTER Many nations are governed by a legislative assembly or parliament. These assemblies often include a group of particularly important government officials, called ministers. The chief minister is often known as the prime ("first") minister or premier. He or she runs the government and sometimes has more power than the head of state.

The name "prime minister" was first used in Great Britain in the 1700's. King George I, who came to the throne in 1714, left most of the business of government to Parliament. Sir Robert Walpole, the strongest minister in Parliament, became leader of the government, instead of the king. For many years since then, the prime minister has been the leader of the *majority* (largest) party in Parliament. One of the greatest British prime ministers was Sir Winston Churchill, who led Britain during World War II.

The British prime minister chooses a special council, or *cabinet*, of minis-

▲ *Indira Gandhi, prime minister of India, who was assassinated by her own Sikh bodyguards on October 31, 1984.*

ters. He or she usually follows their advice. Some strong prime ministers, such as William Gladstone in the 1800's, have acted against the wishes of the cabinet. But if more than half the members of Parliament vote against the prime minister, he or she must resign or call a new election, or both.

Most countries that were once part of the British Empire—such as Canada, Australia, and India—have a parliamentary government run by a prime minister. Some other nations like Spain, Italy, and France have similar governments. The chief minister in these three countries is also called the prime minister.

ALSO READ: CHURCHILL, WINSTON; GEORGE, KINGS OF ENGLAND; GOVERNMENT; PARLIAMENT.

PRINCE EDWARD ISLAND Prince Edward Island is the smallest of the ten Canadian provinces and is one of the four Maritime Provinces. It is about twice the size of Rhode Island, the smallest U.S. state, but its population is much less. The province is small in size, but it is more densely populated than any other Canadian province.

The province is an island in the Gulf of St. Lawrence. Northumber-

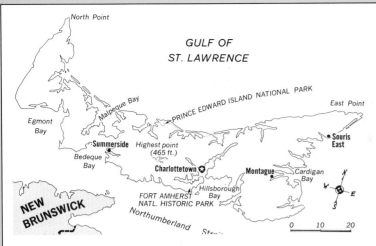

GULF OF
ST. LAWRENCE

North Point

PRINCE EDWARD ISLAND NATIONAL PARK

Malpeque Bay

Egmont
Bay

Summerside

Bedeque
Bay

Highest point
(465 ft.)

Charlottetown

FORT AMHERST
NATL. HISTORIC PARK

East Point

Souris
East

Montague

Cardigan
Bay

Hillsborough
Bay

Northumberland Strait

NEW
BRUNSWICK

N
W   E
S

0   10   20

▲ *Conifer trees stand right by the coastline along Murray Head, on Prince Edward Island.*

◀ *The farmhouse, believed to have been used as a setting for the book* Anne of Green Gables *by Lucy Maud Montgomery, is on Prince Edward Island National Park. It is open to the public.*

▲ *An attractive weatherboard lighthouse keeps vigil for passing ships along Wood Island, one of the many small islets around Prince Edward Island.*

PRINCE EDWARD ISLAND

Capital and largest city
Charlottetown
(15,300 people)

Area
2,180 square miles (5,646 sq. km)

Population
126,646 people

Entry into Confederation
July 1, 1873

Principal river
East River (tidal inlet)

Highest point
Bonshaw Hills
465 feet (142 m)

Famous people
Lucy Maud Montgomery

PROVINCIAL FLOWER

Lady's slipper

The Confederation Chamber in the Provincial Building in Charlottetown, Prince Edward Island, remains furnished as it was in 1864 when the Fathers of Confederation met there to plan the union of Canada. The building is often called the "birthplace of Canada."

land Strait separates it from New Brunswick and Nova Scotia. At its closest point, it is 9 miles (14.5 km) from New Brunswick. Cape Breton Island is to the east.

Prince Edward Island is about 120 miles (195 km) long, with dozens of bays and inlets, high cliffs, and long, sandy beaches. It ranges from about 2 to 35 miles (3 to 55 km) in width. The soil is rich and dark red in color and is ideal for farming. Its climate is kept mild by the ocean surrounding it, and the summer nearly always has fine weather.

About one-third of the island's population is of Scottish descent; one-third is English, one-fifth Irish, and one-sixth French. Some 300 Indians are the only descendants of the original inhabitants.

This province is known for its potatoes and dairy products. Vegetables and flowers grow so well here that the island is known as the "Garden of the Gulf." While farming is the most important occupation on the island, manufacturing and fisheries employ many people. Lobsters and oysters harvested here reach markets in Canada and New England. Silver fox and mink are raised for their fur.

The province is a fine vacation place. Camping, fishing and swimming are enjoyed at Prince Edward Island National Park and in other areas. Deep-sea fishing is excellent, and horse racing, golf, and other holiday activities are popular.

The Micmac Indians first lived on the island. Jacques Cartier, a French explorer, discovered the island on his first voyage to the New World in 1534. The French were the first to colonize it, but it later became British and, in 1873, joined the new nation of Canada.

ALSO READ: CANADA, NEW BRUNSWICK, NOVA SCOTIA.

PRINTING When writing or pictures are reproduced on sheets of paper by contact with an inked surface, we say that the sheets are printed. Printing is one of the world's greatest inventions, for it allows thousands, even millions, of persons to receive information or enjoy works of art. Stories, music, news, business information—all are printed, and modern society needs them all.

Printing was first invented by the Chinese about A.D. 868. Chinese *characters* (symbols that stand for words) were carved onto blocks so that they were raised from the surface. When ink was applied to the raised characters and paper pressed against them, the ink from the raised characters was transferred to the paper. These carved blocks were the first kind of type. Sometime during the A.D. 1000's, the Chinese also invented movable type. Each character was carved on a separate block, so that they could be used over and over in

▼ *Johannes Gutenberg inspects a sheet that has just come from his new printing press. Pages of metal type are fixed in trays and inked by hand (right). Sheets of paper are then placed over the type and pressed down (far right). The press the man is using was an old wine press.*

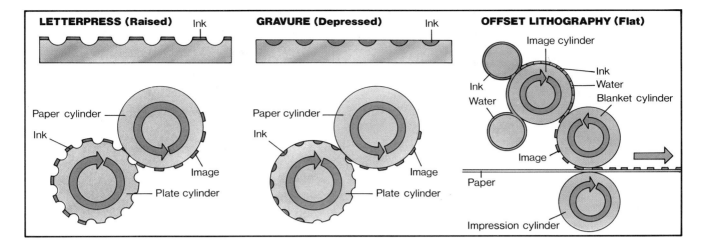

any combination that was needed.

Modern printing began in Europe in the 1450's, when Johannes Gutenberg cast metal *type*, one piece for each letter, in molds. Many letters, exactly alike, could easily be cast for the printer to make into sentences. The old handwritten book was soon replaced, for printing was much faster. A sheet of paper was laid on the type, the press was screwed down, and thousands of letters appeared on the paper at once. Printing was a great help in the "revival of learning" in the Renaissance. Printing presses were quickly established all over Europe and eventually in the American colonies and elsewhere. During the 1800's and 1900's, a great many inventions improved the speed and accuracy of the printing process.

Basic Kinds of Printing There are three basic kinds of printing—*letterpress, gravure* (or *intaglio*), and *lithography*.

Letterpress printing is done with type in which the printing surface is raised above the surface of the metal. The letters are inked with a roller and pressed against paper to make the impression. Letterpress is commonly used for newspapers.

Gravure printing is done with metal plates that have letters or designs set below the surface. These hollowed-out areas are filled with ink, and paper is forced against them with great pressure. This causes the ink to be transferred to the paper. Engraving, a gravure process using deep cuts in the metal, can be seen on wedding invitations and other very formal printed material.

In lithography, the printing surface is neither raised nor sunken. Lithography is based on the principle that grease and water will not mix. If you draw a picture with a crayon, then sprinkle water on it, you will see that the water soaks the paper but makes tight little globs on the wax.

The lettering or other material to be lithographed is put on the printing surface—a metal plate or a special stone—with a greasy substance that attracts a special greasy ink. The sur-

▼ *A big modern color printing press such as this one can print up to 20,000 complete sections of a book or magazine in an hour. This means that more than five big sheets shoot off the press every second the machine is running.*

The first book Gutenberg printed with movable type was probably a Bible, in Latin. It was printed sometime between 1450 and 1456. One of the two copies of the Gutenberg Bible still in existence now belongs to the Smithsonian Institution in Washington, D.C.

► *To print a color picture by offset lithography, it is first photographed through four color filters. Then a printing plate is made for each color. The yellow plate is printed first; then come the magenta and cyan plates. The black is printed last, and the paper then goes through a drying, folding, and cutting unit. It comes out as a finished magazine, newspaper, or book section.*

face is wetted before printing, so that the ink is easily removed from the areas that are not to print. Then the surface is ready for printing. In *offset lithography*, the ink is offset (transferred) to a rubber roller, called a *blanket*, which does the actual printing. This allows the plate to be an inexpensive, thin one, since it is pressing against soft rubber, not against the bed that holds the paper. Photo-offset developed from the use of photography and of the rubber transfer cylinder.

Kinds of Presses   The machine that brings paper into contact with an inked surface to make an *impression* is called a *press*. Presses are very complicated pieces of machinery, and all have different attachments for doing special kinds of jobs. But there are three basic types of press—the *platen*, the *cylinder*, and the *rotary* press.

The platen press has a heavy, flat piece of metal that presses the paper against the inked surface to make an impression. The cylinder press makes an impression by pressing the paper against the inked surface with a large roller, called a cylinder. The rotary press uses a very large cylinder on which several lithographic plates can be attached. As the cylinder revolves, it presses the inked type against the paper and makes an impression.

Cylinder and rotary presses can sometimes print on both sides of the paper at once, in which case they are called *cylinder-perfector* or *rotary-perfector* presses. Some presses are

called *sheet-fed*. This means that paper is put into the press in the form of large sheets. *Web presses* are those that take paper in the form of long continuous rolls (called webs). As the printed paper comes out of the machine, the web press cuts and folds it. Web presses are used in printing newspapers, some kinds of paperback books, and magazines.

Photoengraving   The process of putting pictures into print is called photoengraving. Pictures are usually printed in black and white, in two-color (black plus a second color), or in four-color. Most four-color printing is the combining of the colors red, yellow, blue, and black to make all other possible colors. The three types of photoengraving are *line*, *halftone*, and *color*. Each type is used for certain kinds of pictures.

Line engraving is used to print pictures, such as cartoons, that are composed of lines and have no shading. A photograph is made of the drawing, and the negative is placed on

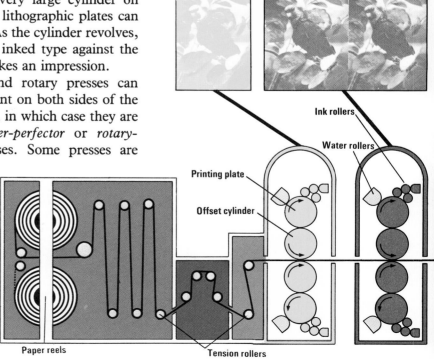

Yellow plate   Magenta plate

Ink rollers

Water rollers

Printing plate

Offset cylinder

Paper reels

Tension rollers

a sheet of light-sensitive metal. When light hits the metal, the surface not covered by the dark parts of the negative goes through a chemical change that makes the surface able to pick up ink. When printed, a copy of the original drawing results.

Halftone engraving is more complicated. It is the method used for printing pictures that do have shading. If you look closely at a newspaper photograph, you will see that the picture is printed with tiny dots. Dark areas of the picture have a heavier concentration of black dots than do the light areas. Shades of gray result from a greater or lesser number of dots. These dots are made by placing a screen of tiny criss-crossed lines over the original picture. When the picture is photographed through the screen, it comes out on the negative as a mass of tiny dots. The dots are transferred to a light-sensitive metal plate, which is then inked and printed.

The color engraving process is similar to that of halftone, except that four separate negatives must be made—one for each basic color—red, yellow, blue, and black. When the metal plates are made (one for each color), the dots show up in a different pattern for each plate. The plate for red, for example, may have a heavier concentration of dots in the middle because more red shows up in the middle of the original picture. On the press, the four plates are inked, each with a separate color. As paper is fed through the press, the color plates print consecutively, on exactly the same place on the paper. The four colors combine in just the right amounts, and the result is a copy of the original.

■ LEARN BY DOING

If you would like to see for yourself how printing is done and how presses work, call your local newspaper. They will probably be glad to make an appointment to show you around. ■

ALSO READ: BOOK; COMMUNICATION; GRAPHIC ARTS; GUTENBURG, JOHAN-

▲ *At the end of the printing process, the printed sheets are folded ready for cutting and binding.*

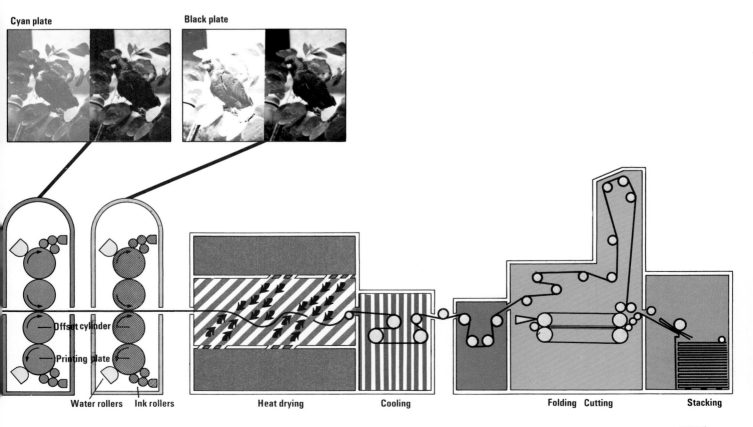

Cyan plate   **Black plate**

Offset cylinder   Printing plate

Water rollers   Ink rollers   Heat drying   Cooling   Folding   Cutting   Stacking

The longest recorded prison sentence in U.S. history was served by Paul Geidel, convicted of second degree murder. When he was released in 1980 he had spent 68 years, eight months, and two days in prison.

The most notorious prison settlement was the French Devil's Island off the coast of French Guiana in South America. It has been estimated that of the 70,000 prisoners deported to Devil's Island only about 2,000 ever returned.

NES; INK; MAGAZINE; NEWSPAPER; PAPER; PUBLISHING; RENAISSANCE; TYPESETTING.

PRISM see COLOR.

PRISON If a person is convicted of a crime, he or she may be locked up in a prison, a special enclosed building that is patrolled by armed guards. A prisoner is separated from the rest of the community and loses the freedom to mix freely with society.

Until the Middle Ages, prisons were reserved for people who had committed major crimes, such as murder. In the 1500's, the courts began to sentence people to prison for committing lesser crimes, such as theft. People were even sent to prison for owing bills they could not pay. Men and women of all ages were herded together in filthy, crowded prisons. They were treated brutally, fed very badly, and were often forced to do hard work. Beginning in the late 1700's, some people began to work to improve conditions in prisons. They tried to make life in prison more bearable. They believed that they could reform criminals. Their beliefs developed into *penology*, the study of prison management and criminal reform.

Although efforts are still being made to improve prisons, many prisoners today still live under crowded conditions, have little to eat, and are sometimes mistreated by other prisoners. A prisoner's activities may be restricted to sleeping in a cell on a small cot, going to the dining hall to eat or outside to a recreation area, and back again to the cell, always under the watchful eye of a guard.

Many prisons today are set up like small cities with laundries, dry cleaners, printing plants, laboratories, and other work areas where prisoners can work and learn a trade or skill. Prisoners may receive some pay for their work. They may work around the prison, doing carpentry, masonry, cooking, electrical work, and farming. Some prisoners are clerks, typists, and dental technicians. Many prisons operate their own factories, where automobile license plates, road signs, and other products used by the state or national government are manufactured. Sometimes, a prison may have schools where prisoners can take high school and college courses. *Psychiatrists* (doctors who treat mental illness) and other counselors may help prisoners with their personal problems. A prisoner with a good behavior record is often given greater freedom and special privileges. One with an excellent record may be made a *trusty* and be allowed to work outside the prison. Trusties may also live in special areas outside the prison. If prisoners behave well over a long period of time, they may be put on *parole*. This means that they will be released before their prison terms have expired, on the condition that they continue to show good behavior.

Much of their prison experience may be seen as preparation for parole. The prisoners are periodically examined to check on their progress. Eventually each prisoner may be eligible to come up before a parole board. The board determines whether or not he or she is sufficiently rehabilitated and not likely to commit another crime. If

▼ *Young inmates, most of them only boys, are exercised in a prison yard in London, England, in the early 1800's. Prisons at that time were often dirty and overcrowded. Imprisonment was the sentence for even very minor offenses.*

this is the case, the board may grant parole. The prisoner is then placed under the supervision of a parole officer, who is based in the prisoner's home community. Before this happens, however, the prisoner must have served a specified period of his or her sentence.

Prisons in the United States are operated by three levels of government. Local jails are run by cities and counties. State prisons are maintained by individual states. Federal penitentiaries are operated by the Federal Government. If a person breaks a city or county law, he or she will go to a city or county jail. Those convicted of violating state and federal laws serve sentences in state or federal prisons. U.S. prisons vary throughout the country. Bad conditions in some prisons have caused prisoners to riot and to fight their guards.

In 1971, one of the worst prison riots in U.S. history occurred at the Attica Correctional Facility in Attica, New York. Mistreatment of prisoners and racial tension were blamed for the riot, in which 32 prisoners and 11 guards were killed. State troopers regained control of the Attica prison after four days. In 1980, another violent uprising occurred at the state penitentiary at Santa Fe, New Mexico. Overcrowding of prisoners was the main cause. This riot left 33 persons dead.

Detention homes are special prisons for people who have committed crimes but are below the legal age at which they can be tried. These prisons are usually *minimum security* prisons. This means that there are fewer guards and fewer restrictions on a prisoner's activities than there would be in most prisons. Detention homes, or reform schools, try to operate like schools and help young people return to the community.

Penologists believe that a prison should not be just a place where criminals are put to be punished. Imprisonment should also help to *rehabilitate* those who are serving their sentences. Rehabilitation means that prisoners

are helped to become better people, so that when they leave prison they may get jobs and not commit crimes again.

ALSO READ: CRIME, JUVENILE DELINQUENCY, MURDER, TRIAL.

PRIVATEERS see PIRATES AND PRIVATEERS.

PROBLEM SOLVING see REASONING, SCIENCE.

PROGRAM, COMPUTER see COMPUTER.

PROHIBITION The word "prohibit" means to forbid something. The term "prohibition" in U.S. history has usually meant a law forbidding the making and selling of alcoholic drinks. Many American states passed prohibition laws during the 1800's. In 1919, Congress passed the Eighteenth Amendment to the Constitution of the United States. It prohibited the manufacture and sale of all alcoholic drinks. A famous national prohibition law called the Volstead Act was passed in that year to enforce

▲ *The storming of the Bastille, a fortress-prison in Paris, on July 14, 1789, marked the start of the French Revolution.*

There are about 30 times more men in prisons than there are women.

▲ *Carry A. Nation, an early prohibitionist, holds two of the weapons she used in her fight against whiskey—a Bible she used in preaching to those who drank, and a hatchet for wrecking saloons.*

It is said that Al Capone, the gangster and bootlegger who made and sold liquor during Prohibition in the United States, made 60 million dollars a year from his illegal activities. Al Capone's gang killed seven members of a rival bootlegging gang on St. Valentine's Day, 1929. This became known as the St. Valentine's Day Massacre.

▲ *Sergei Prokofiev, Russian composer.*

and regulate the Eighteenth Amendment. The people who supported the Volstead Act hoped it would stop people from drinking.

But drinking was not stopped. Illegal drinking places called "speakeasies" opened. Gangsters made huge amounts of money buying, making, and selling illegal liquor. Some people made their own liquor at home. A great deal of liquor was smuggled in from other countries. Also, the government lost millions of dollars in liquor taxes. In 1933, Congress passed the Twenty-first Amendment, which repealed the Eighteenth Amendment. Making and selling alcoholic drinks was then no longer against the law.

ALSO READ: ALCOHOLIC BEVERAGE.

PROKOFIEV, SERGEI (1891–1953) Have you ever heard the story of *Peter and the Wolf* set to music? This unique musical work was created by the Russian composer, Sergei Prokofiev. The characters in the tale are played by instruments of the orchestra. Peter, a little boy who sets out to catch a wolf, is played by the violins. Peter's grandfather, who tries to keep Peter from catching the wolf, is played by a bassoon. Peter has two companions who help him—a duck (played by a oboe) and a bird (played by a flute). The wolf that Peter catches is played by French horns. And the three hunters who help take the wolf to the zoo are played by trumpets and trombones. During a performance of *Peter and the Wolf*, a narrator tells the story as the orchestra plays the various parts.

Prokofiev was born on a country estate at Sontsovka (now called Krasnoye) in southern Russia. His mother was his first music teacher and encouraged him to start studying music at a very early age. He quickly became a skilled pianist and began composing music. By the time he was nine years old, Prokofiev had already

written a three-act opera entitled *The Giant.* Prokofiev was admitted to the St. Petersburg Conservatory of Music at age 13. He graduated seven years later with high honors. When he was 23, Prokofiev won the Rubinstein Prize (a high award for excellence in muscial composition) for his *First Piano Concerto*.

Prokofiev's music is modern in form and sound. His *Classical Symphony* for a small orchestra was written as if an earlier composer, such as Mozart, were writing music in the 1900's. *The Love for Three Oranges* was written for the Chicago Opera Company.

Prokofiev left Russia at the outbreak of the revolution in 1917, living in exile in the United States and France. In 1933, he returned with his family to settle in the Soviet Union. In 1948, Prokofiev and other leading Soviet musicians were accused by Soviet authorities of composing music that was "distorted" and not appropriate for Soviet citizens to listen to. Despite this censure, Prokofiev continued to compose until his death in Moscow in 1953. The Communist Party finally changed its opinion of Prokofiev's music. His *Ninth Symphony* was awarded the Lenin Prize in 1958.

ALSO READ: COMPOSER, MUSIC, MUSICAL INSTRUMENTS, OPERA, ORCHESTRAS AND BANDS.

PROMETHEUS Prometheus was a hero in Greek myths. He belonged to the Titans, a race of gods.

Prometheus often helped *mortals* (ordinary people, as opposed to gods). He stole fire from the gods and gave it to the human race. This angered Zeus, the leader of the gods. He had Prometheus chained to a rock. Each day an eagle came and tore out his liver. Every night Zeus made the liver grow back again. Prometheus could have brought his suffering to an end by telling Zeus a certain secret, but Prometheus courageously refused to do this. Because of this, he was one of the great mythological heroes to mankind. Finally Hercules, a famous Greek hero, killed the eagle and freed Prometheus.

ALSO READ: HERCULES, PANDORA.

PRONOUN see PARTS OF SPEECH.

PRONUNCIATION When you speak a language, you are pronouncing it. The particular way in which you speak it is called pronunciation. Perhaps you have noticed that people from different areas of the United States pronounce words differently. In many so-called southern accents and the Bostonian accent, the "r" sound is replaced by an "ah" sound. "Larger" is pronounced "lahjah," and "garden" is pronounced "gahden." People in some places pronounce "oily" as "early" and "early" as "oily."

English pronunciation also differs in different parts of the world. For example, many British people pronounce "been" as "bean," "secretary" as "secratree," and "better" as "bet-tah." The Australian English pronunciation of "mate," "race," and "pail" would sound like "might," "rice," and "pile" to someone from the United States.

The pronunciation of languages keeps changing because the people who speak them keep changing. The word "been," for example, was pronounced "bin" or "ben" by English people in the 1600's. English settlers in the New World also pronounced "been" as "bin" or "ben." But American settlers became cut off from the everyday speech of people in England. Today, the British pronunciation of "been" has changed to "bean," while the American pronunciation has remained "bin" or "ben,"

just as it was in England in the 1600's.

The English language has no strict set of rules for correct pronunciation. But if you pronounce words too differently from everyone else, people will have a hard time understanding you. People usually adapt their pronunciation to the way others around them are speaking. In studying a foreign language, you must learn to pronounce words in a new way. If you use American English pronunciation when speaking French, for example, French people will not be able to understand you easily. If a French person speaks English totally with French pronunciation, you will probably not be able to understand him or her.

The best way to find out the correct pronunciation of a word is to look it up in a dictionary. Each entry word is respelled in a special way, often using special letters and markings, to show you how it is pronounced. The *pronunciation key* is at the front of the dictionary.

ALSO READ: DICTIONARY, ENGLISH LANGUAGE, LANGUAGES, SPEECH.

PROPAGANDA Propaganda is a way of attempting to change public opinion through written or spoken messages. Propaganda presents only one side of an issue. Its purpose is to persuade people to have a favorable opinion of that viewpoint. People are subjected to propaganda every day through television, radio, movies, magazines, newspapers, books, and posters. Propaganda is used by and for individuals, businesses, religious groups, political organizations, and governments. When propaganda is honestly used, it is a fair method of presenting one viewpoint, with facts to back it up, to the public. When propaganda is misused, it twists facts and presents inaccurate information.

Industries and other special-interest groups use propaganda

Listen to how you pronounce "Mary," "marry," and "merry." Most Americans think that these words are *homonyms*, words that sound the same but have different meanings. British people, however, pronounce each of these words differently.

The British writer George Bernard Shaw claimed that, according to pronunciation rules of English, "ghoti" could be pronounced "fish." Say *gh* as in "rough," *o* as in "women," and *ti* as in "nation," and you will see what he meant.

▲ *The propaganda war of the early 1960's. An electric billboard flashes news from West Berlin into East Berlin.*

▼ *One of the most influential forms of propaganda in modern times was the little red book of "Quotations from the Works of Mao Tse-tung," in China. Here, young Chinese bandsmen hold up their little red books as a gesture of loyalty. In the late 1960s all Chinese had to have a copy—making it probably the highest printed publication ever (after the Bible).*

through advertising and other kinds of public relations. When a company advertises its products, it tries to make you want to use them. So the company tells you only the good things about its products. For example, the manufacturers of a detergent will tell you only how well the detergent cleans, how good it smells, and how cheap it is. They will *not* tell you that the detergent may pollute the water.

During elections, political parties use propaganda in publicity campaigns to persuade people to vote for their candidates. In wartime, nations use propaganda to convince their own citizens that the war is necessary. Nations also use propaganda to try to persuade the enemy to give up. In peacetime, nations use propaganda to persuade their citizens and the rest of the world that the government's actions are right.

Everyone is exposed to a great deal of propaganda. An individual should form an opinion only after hearing both sides of an issue, not just what one side chooses to make public. Propaganda is a useful method of persuasion. But if citizens do not think independently, propaganda can be a very dangerous tool.

ALSO READ: ADVERTISING, PUBLIC RELATIONS.

▲ *A French disinfectant manufacturer combined advertising and propaganda by showing Premier Georges Clemenceau using the firm's product on a captive Germany after World War I.*

PROPAGATION see PLANT, REPRODUCTION.

PROPHET A prophet is a person believed to have powers of knowing the future. Great kings once employed prophets to advise them on personal and government problems. Much ancient pagan prophecy was based on the idea of *fate*, which caused everything to happen, or on the idea that gods and spirits control everything that happens in the world. Prophets were considered to be the "keepers of secret wisdom" by which they were able to know of things to come.

All primitive peoples have had *sha-*

mans (witch doctors or medicine men) who were believed to be able to contact the spirits and know the future. The ancient Greeks had prophetesses called *sibyls* or *oracles* who were located at the temples of various gods and goddesses. Babylonian prophets, called *magi*, predicted the future by gazing into crystal balls or by astrology (reading the stars). The prophets of ancient Rome, called *augurs*, predicted events by "reading" the entrails (internal organs) of dead animals. According to legend, one augur warned Julius Caesar to "beware the Ides [the fifteenth] of March." On that day, Caesar was murdered.

Prophets throughout the world have tried to predict the future by watching for *omens*. Omens were things that happened in nature, such as a dark cloud appearing at a certain place or a particular bird flying in a certain direction. People believed these omens were signs or warnings of future events. For this reason, we speak of "weather prophets," meaning persons who attempt to tell what the weather will be, even though they use no magic to do so.

The Hebrew and Islamic prophets differed from the pagan ones in several ways. They believed in a single, all-powerful God rather than in many gods or spirits. Instead of using crystal balls, entrails, or astrology, they regarded themselves as directly inspired by God. And, unlike the pagans, they were concerned with eternal principles of good and evil, not with what certain gods happened to want at the moment.

Feeling as they did, the Hebrew and Islamic prophets preached the word of God, reminding people of His laws and threatening with punishment those who did not obey. They foretold the future when a person or nation was to be punished, but were more concerned with urging people to reform.

Some of the best-known Hebrew prophets were Isaiah, Jeremiah,

Ezekiel, Daniel, Jonah, Hosea, and Amos. Their prophecies are contained in the Old Testament of the Bible. Fulfillment of many of those prophecies, Christians believe, can be found in the New Testament. Muhammad was the great prophet of Islam. His writings are contained in the Koran.

ALSO READ: ASTROLOGY, BIBLE, FORTUNE-TELLING, GODS AND GODDESSES, KORAN, MAGIC, RELIGION, SUPERSTITION, WITCHCRAFT.

▲ *The theater at Delphi, site of the great Greek shrine to the god Apollo. The Greeks had prophetesses, called oracles, at their chief holy places. The oracle at Delphi was one of the best known of these.*

PROTECTIVE COLORING The next time you walk in the woods or fields, look around very carefully. You may be surprised at the number of animals you can spot in the trees and shadows! Many animals have a color or a pattern of colors that matches their surroundings and protects them from enemies. A color pattern that protects an animal is called protective coloration, or protective coloring.

The back of a fawn has broad stripes of two shades of brown. White spots speckle the brown. When a fawn lies down on the floor of the forest, its stripes and spots look almost exactly like the pattern made by sunlight shining through the leaves of trees and bushes. People or other animals can look at a fawn without realizing they are seeing anything but the sun-speckled ground. This is an example of protective coloring.

Chameleons can change the color of their skin to match their different surroundings. Their skin has cells which contain colored pigments. Some cells have black pigment, others have red or yellow. A Chameleon needs this protective coloring because it remains in one place for a long time, waiting for prey to come close enough, so it can catapult its sticky tongue and seize its victim.

PROTECTIVE COLORING

▲ *The large leaf insects of Asia are slow-moving creatures that look like the leaves on which they live.*

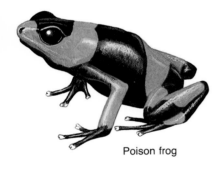

Poison frog

Cinnabar moth caterpillar

Hoverfly

▲ *The bright colors of the South American poison frog warn predators that it should be avoided. The cinnabar moth caterpillar and the harmless hoverfly both mimic a wasp's coloring for protection, because birds will avoid wasps.*

Animals of all kinds—insects, fishes, amphibians, reptiles, birds, and mammals—have protective coloring. There are insects that look like leaves, twigs, tree bark, berries, and flowers. One side of a flounder looks like the sand on which it usually lies. Quail spend much of their time on the ground, seeking seeds and berries. On their backs are brown, black, and white feathers that have a pattern like the ground and its covering of dead grass and weeds. This protective coloring makes it very hard for flying hawks to see quail on the ground.

A few animals, such as the chameleon (a small lizard), can change their coloring to match their surroundings. Some animals that live in snowy regions change the color of their fur or feathers in the winter. The ptarmigan (a kind of grouse) and the snowshoe rabbit are white in the winter but dull brown the rest of the year.

For an animal to be protected by its color, the animal should not be moving. A kallima butterfly standing on a twig looks exactly like a brown, dried leaf. But when the kallima flies, a bird can easily tell that the butterfly is not a dead leaf being blown by the wind.

Very young animals usually cannot move very fast. This makes it hard for them to escape their enemies. Instead of trying to escape, they hide. To hide well, young animals have a special need for protective coloring. Many are born with protective colors. Newly hatched ostriches are the color of

the sand on which ostriches live. When danger approaches, baby ostriches "freeze" and remain motionless so that their enemies will not see them. Newly hatched eels are as colorless as the water in which they swim.

One kind of protective coloring is called *mimicry*. An animal that cannot defend itself against its enemies, mimics (looks like) a similar animal that can defend itself. Hawk moths, which have no stings, mimic bumblebees, which do have stings. Birds learn not to eat monarch butterflies because they make the birds sick. Birds could safely eat viceroy butterflies. But the viceroy mimics the monarch. So birds do not eat the viceroy, either.

Protective coloring is the result of *natural selection*. A good example of the way natural selection works is shown by a certain kind of moth that lives in Britain. In 1850, most of these moths were light-colored, but some were dark. A hundred years later, in the same region, there were more dark-colored moths than light-colored ones. What had happened? Many factories had been built. Smoke from the factories darkened walls and tree trunks. Birds easily saw the light-colored moths on the darkened walls and trees. But they could not easily see the dark-colored moths. Birds ate

▼ *Ptarmigans change color with the seasons to blend with the color of the land.*

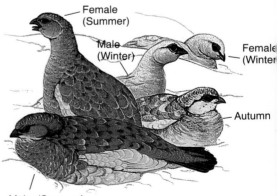

Female (Summer)

Male (Winter)

Female (Winter)

Autumn

Male (Summer)

more light-colored moths than dark-colored moths. More dark-colored moths lived long enough to lay eggs. So, there came to be more dark-colored moths. The dark color had become a protective coloring.

ALSO READ: ANIMAL DEFENSES, CAMOUFLAGE, EVOLUTION, FEATHER, FUR.

PROTEIN Protein is a very important food material. Meat, fish, milk, cheese, cereals, and certain vegetables contain protein. Besides being a food, protein is one of the most important of all the substances that make up plants and animals. Protein is the active part of *protoplasm*, which is the living material of plant and animal cells. Enzymes, some hormones, antigens, and antibodies are proteins. Your body contains thousands of different proteins.

Proteins are huge molecules made up of thousands of atoms. All protein molecules have nitrogen, carbon, hydrogen, and oxygen atoms. In addition, many protein molecules contain sulfur, and some have iodine atoms. Each protein is a chain of chemical building blocks called *amino acids*. There are many kinds of amino acids, but only about 20 are found often in proteins. When amino acids join together, they release a molecule of water and form a bond. Different combinations of amino acids form different kinds of proteins, each with a different structure.

Some of the amino acids necessary for human life must be obtained from food. The exact number depends on a person's age and health. Good protein foods are those that contain all the necessary acids. Meat and cheese are two good protein foods. Gelatin is a poor protein food. It lacks some of the needed amino acids. The digestive juices in your stomach and small intestine break up food proteins into amino acids. These pass through the walls of your intestine and enter your bloodstream. Your blood carries the amino acids to the cells that make up the tissues of your body. The cells link together the amino acids to make new proteins.

ALSO READ: CELL, FOOD, HORMONE, HUMAN BODY, NUTRITION.

PROTESTANT CHURCHES
The Protestant churches are branches of Christianity. All of these groups grew out of the Protestant Reformation of the 1500's, which broke away from the religious ideas and practices of the Roman Catholic Church. They have many basic beliefs in common, but they differ from each other in certain beliefs and rituals. Throughout the world there are over 338 million Protestants.

A branch of Protestantism called Lutheranism was started in the 1500's. Other Protestant groups were formed in England and Switzerland around the same time. Some of the major Protestant denominations today are the Presbyterian, Episcopal, Methodist, Baptist, and Lutheran churches. The Disciples of Christ, the United Church of Christ, and the Latter-day Saints (Mormons) also have large memberships. The Society of Friends (Quakers) and Adventists are other Protestant groups.

Most Protestants believe that the Bible is the word of God. They follow its teachings as their religious law, but most of them are free to interpret (understand) it as they wish. This is one of the reasons why there are so many different Protestant churches. The groups that believe in accepting every word of the Bible without question are called *fundamentalists*.

Unlike Roman Catholicism, which has a pope, Protestantism does not have a single leader. Protestants often elect officers of regional and national councils of their churches. The head of the national group is called by various names in different denomina-

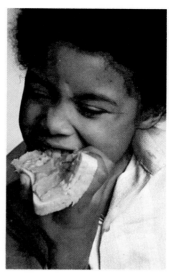

▲ *Proteins are not only found in meat and milk products. Peanuts, shown here in the form of peanut butter, are a good source of protein.*

An adult needs about 2 ounces (60 grams) of protein every day to replace protein lost by wear and tear of the body.

▲ *The Old West Church in Calais, Vermont, is a typical New England Protestant church.*

tions, such as bishop, general secretary, or president. Protestant churches sponsor social welfare work in the United States and other countries. Missionary groups have started hospitals and schools in many parts of the world where education and medical care were once nonexistent.

A main idea in Protestantism is the "priesthood of believers." Protestants believe that people can communicate with God through their own faith instead of only through the aid of sacraments given by a priest. Church services are led by a *minister*. Protestant ministers may marry and have families. Lay people (members who are not ministers) take part in services and church government. In recent years, women have been ordained as ministers in a number of Protestant churches for the first time.

Much work has been done to try to bring the Protestant churches togeth-

er. Many U.S. Protestant denominations belong to the National Council of the Churches of Christ. Protestant churches all over the world, including Orthodox Eastern churches, joined in forming the World Council of Churches in 1948. Several individual Protestant churches have joined others in mergers. The United Church of Canada is made up of several churches. Three branches of the Methodist Church joined each other in 1939. The Congregational Christian and the Evangelical and Reformed churches formed the United Church of Christ in 1961. A few Protestant churches have split, and new churches have been formed.

ALSO READ: CHRISTIANITY; JESUS CHRIST; LUTHER, MARTIN; PROTESTANT REFORMATION; RELIGION; ROMAN CATHOLIC CHURCH, SOCIETY OF FRIENDS.

LEADING PROTESTANT GROUPS IN THE UNITED STATES

Group	Membership	Established*	Headquarters
Baptist churches			
American Baptist Churches in the U.S.A.	1,568,778	1907	Valley Forge, Pennsylvania
National Baptist Convention, U.S.A., Inc.	5,500,000	1880	Baton Rouge, Louisiana
National Baptist Convention of America	2,668,799	1880	Little Rock, Arkansas
Southern Baptist Convention	14,722,617	1845	Nashville, Tennessee
Christian Church (Disciples of Christ)	1,086,668	1804	Indianapolis, Indiana
Christian Churches and Churches of Christ	1,071,995	1811	Cincinnati, Ohio
Church of Christ, Scientist (Christian Scientists)	no figure available	1879	Boston, Massachusetts
Church of Jesus Christ of Latter-Day Saints (Mormon)	4,000,000	1830	Salt Lake City, Utah
Church of the Nazarene	543,762	1908	Kansas City, Missouri
Episcopal Church of the U.S.A.	2,462,300	1789	New York, New York
Jehovah's Witnesses	773,219	1884	Brooklyn, New York
Lutheran churches			
American Lutheran Church	2,339,946	1960	Minneapolis, Minnesota
Lutheran Church in America	2,910,281	1962	New York, New York
Lutheran Church—Missouri Synod	2,628,133	1847	St. Louis, Missouri
Methodist churches			
African Methodist Episcopal Church	2,210,000	1816	Washington, D.C.
African Methodist Episcopal Zion Church	1,202,229	1796	Washington, D.C.
Christian Methodist Episcopal Church	466,718	1870	Chicago, Illinois
United Methodist Church	9,291,936	1968	New York, New York
Orthodox Church in America	1,000,000	1792	New York, New York
Pentecostal churches			
Assemblies of God	2,160,667	1914	Springfield, Missouri
Church of God (Cleveland, Tennessee)	505,775	1886	Cleveland, Tennessee
United Pentecostal Church	500,000	1945	Hazlewood, Missouri
Presbyterian churches			
Presbyterian Church in the United States	866,500	1861	Atlanta, Georgia
United Presbyterian Church in the U.S.A.	3,092,151	1958	Philadelphia, Pennsylvania
Salvation Army, The	434,002	1865	New York, New York
Seventh-day Adventists	638,929	1863	Washington, D.C.
United Church of Christ	1,662,568	1957	New York, New York

*Recent dates show that two or more churches have merged.

PROTESTANT REFORMATION

In Europe in the 1500's, a great religious movement called the Reformation took place. Its aim was to reform, or change, the ways of the Roman Catholic Church. The movement ended with the forming of the Protestant churches.

Early Stirrings of Rebellion Although the Reformation officially began in 1517, its roots probably go back hundreds of years before that. The Roman Catholic Church was the established church and the most powerful force in Europe. Its popes were even stronger than kings. The popes, kings, and nobles constantly fought with one another over territory. Here and there, people began to question the power of the Catholic popes. One of the first to speak out against the Church was a French merchant, Peter Waldo, in the 1100's. In England, a scholar and priest named John Wycliffe preached against the Catholic Church from 1368 to 1374. Wycliffe's followers translated the Bible into English. In Bohemia, John Huss was burned at the stake in 1415 for heresy (disagreeing with the official beliefs of the Church). The rebirth of learning in the 1400's brought education to more people. Rebellion grew. Many people wanted Christianity to return to its early ways of simple devotion to God. They were angered by the greed and misbehavior of some of the Roman Catholic clergy.

The Reformation Begins In 1517, a monk named Martin Luther posted 95 theses (statements of belief) on a church door in Wittenberg, Germany. In them, he attacked the authority of the pope and many of the practices of the Catholic Church. His followers, the Lutherans, became the first Protestants. Switzerland had two famed Protestant reformers. Ulrich Zwingli led the movement in Zurich in the 1520's. In 1536, in Geneva, John Calvin began to teach Protestant ideas. Calvin had fled from France to escape punishment for his beliefs. He was especially noted for putting Protestant thought into a clear and orderly form. Luther and Calvin are often called the "Fathers of the Reformation."

King Henry VIII of England broke away from the Catholic Church in 1534. Pope Clement VII had refused to annul (cancel) the king's first marriage so that he could marry Anne Boleyn. The king announced that from that time on he, not the pope, would be the head of the Church of England. Henry's daughter, Mary Tudor, as queen, tried to make England Catholic again and burned many Protestant leaders at the stake. Queen Elizabeth I brought Protestantism back to England in 1563. Another Protestant leader was John Knox of Scotland. Knox helped force Mary, Queen of Scots (a Catholic), to give up her throne and leave her country.

Last Years of the Reformation The Catholic Church did not allow Protestantism to spread without a harsh struggle. It created its own *Counter Reformation*. It called the Council of

▲ *John Calvin was a French theologian whose original name was Jean Chauvin. In later years he used a Latin version of the name,* Calvinus. *His strict form of Protantism became known as Calvinism.*

▼ *Leaders of the Roman Catholic Church met at the Council of Trent between 1545 and 1563. One of its chief purposes was to get rid of the slack practices of the Church that Martin Luther had criticized.*

▲ *A scene during the Massacre of St. Bartholomew's Day in 1572, when some 29,000 French Protestants were murdered.*

In 1976, the Episcopal Church in the United States voted that women might be ordained (certified) as priests. Before that, women had always been excluded from the priesthood.

Trent in 1545 to find a means of stopping the revolution and of bringing self-reform. Despite this, strife between Catholics and Protestants continued. In 1572, Calvin's followers in France, the Huguenots, were murdered by the thousands. A savage religious conflict was fought in Germany and nearby countries from 1618 to 1648. It was called the Thirty Years' War. Over half of all the German people died in it. The Reformation accomplished many of its aims. The Roman Catholic Church no longer ruled without question. Protestant churches were established in many parts of Europe. People began to think of themselves as individuals, with the right to make their own decisions and choose their own beliefs. Out of this new found freedom of thought came a growth in scholarship and the scientific achievements of such thinkers as Galileo and Newton. There was an increase in concern with the material world—with life on earth rather than life after death.

ALSO READ: HENRY, KINGS OF ENGLAND; LUTHER, MARTIN; PROTESTANT CHURCHES; ROMAN CATHOLIC CHURCH.

PROTIST Protists are very small and simple living things. Most plants and animals have many cells and many different kinds of cells. These cells are separated into groups called *tissues*. Each tissue is made up of the same kind of cells. Protists are not divided into tissues. Some protists have only one cell. Other protists have many cells, but all their cells are very much alike.

There are *lower protists* and *higher protists*. The lower protists include bacteria and blue-green algae. The higher protists include all the other algae and the protozoa and fungi. Algae, bacteria, and fungi are plants. Protozoa are animals. So, protists can be either plants or animals.

In 1886, a German biologist, Ernst Haeckel, was the first to suggest using the name "protist" for a group of plants and animals. He suggested it because biologists were having trouble placing fungi and one-celled plants and animals in proper groups in the plant and animal kingdoms. For example, some one-celled living things have cell walls and contain chlorophyll, as plants do. They also move about under their own power, as animals do. Are they plants or animals? Haeckel thought that by making a separate group—the pro-

▼ *The lower protists include blue-green algae, shown here as they appear under a microscope.*

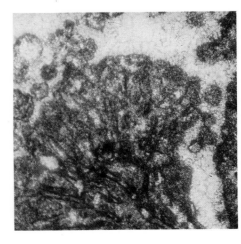

tists—he would solve the problem. Haeckel's idea of protists is not accepted by biologists today. They say that the group includes too many unrelated organisms. But the word is still used for one-celled organisms.

ALSO READ: ALGAE, ANIMAL, CELL, FUNGUS, PLANT, PROTOZOAN.

PROTOPLASM see CELL.

PROTOZOAN A protozoan is an extremely tiny form of animal life. Most protozoa can be seen only under a microscope, but some larger ones grow to be a quarter or a half inch (6 to 12 mm) long. There are more than 30,000 different kinds of protozoa, and they live anywhere there is water.

Protozoa by the billions dart through pond and sea water. Other kinds move among the tiny grains of moist soil in a garden. Some are parasites that live inside the bodies of plants and animals. A small puddle of rainwater, left alone for just a few hours, will have a population of protozoa numbering in the thousands. Protozoa come in many shapes. Some look like round balls, and others are long and thin. They may be shaped like bells or like spirals. Certain protozoa in the ocean grow delicate shells and look like tiny snails.

Protozoa are different from other animals in many ways. Protozoa are made of only one cell. Other animals contain many kinds of cells. Some protozoa contain *chlorophyll*, a substance usually found only in plants. Because protozoa are so different from other animals, many scientists think protozoa should not be classified as either plant or animal, but should belong to another special group. This special group is called *protists* or *protista*.

The cell of a protozoan is made up of a lump of living material called *protoplasm*. Inside the protoplasm, a *nucleus* controls the animal's movements and actions. If the nucleus is destroyed, the protozoan dies. Some kinds of protozoa have more than one nucleus, even hundreds of them. Protozoa must have water to live in. Some are so small, however, that a tiny film of water between two grains of desert sand can be enough for them to survive.

Protozoa get food in several ways. Some absorb dissolved food through the membrane that surrounds their cell of protoplasm. Some protozoa, such as *didiniums*, actually chase and capture their food. Another protozoan, the *amoeba*, can push a part of its body forward to cover and trap its prey. Most protozoa eat tiny particles of living matter. They may feed on bacteria, yeasts, algae, and other protozoa.

Protozoa reproduce by dividing. They split themselves to make two new single-celled animals, each with its own nucleus. Some protozoa produce their offspring on stalks attached to their bodies. A little budlike projection forms and grows. Then the new protozoa split off and start their own lives.

Many protozoa cannot move around under their own power but must depend on the movements of the water. A group of protozoa called *flagellates*

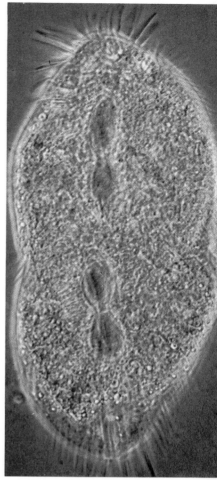

▲ *In this microphotograph, a protozoan is shown as it is beginning to narrow in the middle before it splits into two new cells. The nucleus has already divided.*

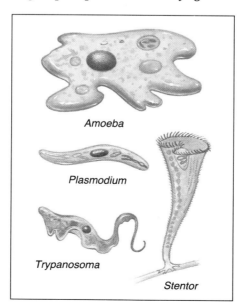

Amoeba

Plasmodium

Trypanosoma

Stentor

◀ *Four protozoans:* Amoebas *are jellylike animals that constantly change their shape.* Trypanosoma *and* Plasmodium *are dangerous to humans—*Trypanosoma *causes sleeping sickness;* Plasmodium *is the malaria parasite.* Stentor *uses its* cilia *(tiny hairs) to beat the water. This creates currents which help to bring it food.*

▲ *This protozoan is a radiolarian. Long, fine threads of protoplasm, stiffened and protected by silica, stand out from the rest of its cell. When radiolarians die, the silica in their cells falls to the sea floor and eventually forms a rocklike deposit.*

There are more than 65,000 psychologists in the United States and more than 27,000 psychiatrists.

are able to move around on their own. They are equipped with a whiplike projection that lashes rapidly back and forth to move the protozoan along. Other protozoa have *cilia*, projections that look like tiny hairs. The cilia move through the water like rows of oars. Still other protozoa (such as the amoeba) creep or flow around by moving the protoplasm in their soft bodies.

The protozoa that normally live in human bodies are harmless, but some kinds of protozoa can cause disease in people, animals, and plants. Malaria is caused by a group of parasitic protozoa called *plasmodia*. One type of amoeba causes a serious disease called *amoebic dysentery*. Sleeping sickness is caused by any of various parasitic protozoa, called *trypanosomes*.

ALSO READ: ANIMAL, ANIMAL KINGDOM, CELL, DISEASE, PARASITE, PROTIST.

PSYCHOLOGY Have you ever wondered how your mind works? Where do ideas come from? Why are some people quiet, while others are very talkative? Why do some things make you feel happy, while other things make you sad? What causes you to choose one object or action over other possible choices? These are the kinds of questions that the science of psychology tries to answer. Psychologists study the *minds* and *behavior* of people.

The mind is hard to describe. It is the total of all activities carried on in that part of the brain called the *cerebrum*. Your mind consists of all the ideas, thoughts, feelings, experiences, and memories that you have had, and how you think and feel about them. Your behavior is how you act as a result of what goes on in the world around you. When you hear something that you think is funny, you laugh. Laughing is a kind of behavior, and so are crying, fighting, humming a tune, tapping a finger, gritting teeth, or sleeping.

Mind and Behavior Mind and behavior are two important ingredients that make up a person. To learn more about mind and behavior, psychologists study *perception, learning, motivation*, and *personality*.

PERCEPTION. When you see a fire with your eyes, you *perceive* it. Your eyes send a signal to your brain telling you the fire is there. Human beings perceive things through the senses of sight, hearing, touch, taste, and smell. Through these senses, you gather information about the world around you. The mind then sorts out the information so that you can understand it.

LEARNING. When information enters your mind through your senses, the first thing you do is try to understand the information. Babies, for example, may think fire is pretty when they see it. But when they try to touch it, they get burned. In this way, the babies have learned what fire is like—it's pretty, but also hot! Learning can take place in several ways. Psychologists investigate all the ways of learning to find out which ways work best in various situations. They also study how people use what they learned in the past in order to learn new things.

MOTIVATION. What makes people do things? Or what makes people want to do things? You have probably heard of police detectives who ask, "What's the *motive* for the crime?" They are asking a psychological question: What is the motivation? *Why* did the criminal do what he or she did? Let's say you decide to buy an ice-cream cone. You could be motivated to buy it by several things. Perhaps you are hungry. It may be a hot day and you want something to make you feel cool. Maybe someone asked you to buy the ice cream, or maybe you are buying it as a surprise for someone.

Quite often, people do not know or understand why they do certain things. Have you ever felt angry and gotten mad at someone but couldn't explain *why* you got mad? You must have had a reason or motivation, but you didn't know what it was. A boy may buy an ice-cream because he thinks he's hungry. But his real motivation (the motivation that he's not aware of) may be a wish to make others jealous. Television advertisements are designed to motivate people to do certain things—usually to buy products. Psychologists study people's motivations to find out how they affect behavior and personality.

PERSONALITY. When you say that someone is a grouchy person, a popular person, a shy person, a business-like person, a funny person, or a nervous person, you are talking about his or her personality. Your personality is that part of your behavior that you show to other people. The words "person" and "personality" come from the latin word *persona*. In ancient Rome, a persona was the mask that an actor wore on stage.

Your personality is a kind of mask that you wear when you are with other people. Personality is the part of your mind and behavior by which other people know you. There is much of your mind, however, that no one ever knows. It stays deep inside you. When you look at the ocean, you can see the waves and breakers and whatever else is on the surface. But the surface is only one small part of a very big, deep, and often mysterious body of water. Your personality is like the surface of the ocean. It is only one small part of your whole mind. Psychologists try to solve the mysteries of what the mind is and how it works.

Branches of Psychology The science of psychology is divided into several specialties. *Experimental psychologists* do laboratory research on humans and animals to find out how

the senses work and what causes behavior. The *psychology of learning* studies how people learn—how they get ideas and how they put ideas to use. One field of learning psychology is *educational psychology* that studies the problems of learning in schools. *Child psychologists* study the growth and development of babies and young people. Their research has been helpful in guiding parents, teachers, medical doctors, counselors, and others who work with young people and need to understand them.

The *psychology of individual differences* tries to discover why people act alike or differently from each other. Psychologists in this field have created many kinds of tests to find out a person's individual characteristics. For example, some tests measure your interests—what you like or don't like to do. Some are intelligence tests that measure how well you can learn certain things as compared with everyone else of your age or background. Some tests measure *aptitudes*—the things that you have a talent for or are likely to do well in. Other tests measure personality, achievement (what you have learned so far), and attitudes (your opinions about things). These tests are used by many people—teachers, counselors, and job interviewers—to determine who you are and what your strengths and weaknesses may be.

▲ *Psychologists are concerned with human behavior and with what makes people happy or sad. Here a psychologist counsels a young woman who is in an upset state of mind.*

▼ *How and what a young child draws may reveal to a psychologist how well that child gets along with other young people.*

▲ *A simple conversation between a psychologist and a patient in the privacy of a quiet office can be very revealing and can give the psychologist much to work on.*

Medical researchers have found that the mind and body are not really independent of each other. If you are physically ill, you probably cannot think in the same way as you do when you are healthy. If you worry too much about something, you can become physically ill.

Abnormal psychology is the study of mental or emotional problems. Psychologists try to find out the causes of these problems and suggest ways of working them out. Psychiatrists work very closely with psychologists. *Psychiatrists* are actually medical doctors who specialize in mental illness. They treat mentally ill people in hospitals or in their offices. Psychiatrists, psychologists, and psychological counselors all work together to improve methods of treatment.

Social psychologists study the behavior of people in groups. They are interested in how groups of people treat each other in different situations, and they study how one group behaves toward another group. For example, a social psychologist would be interested in studying how a group of sixth graders behaves toward a group of third or fourth graders. *Personnel* and *industrial psychologists* deal with people at their jobs. Industrial psychologists use tests to find out what kind of job a person is suited for. They also help workers who may not be satisfied with their jobs, who are having trouble doing their work, or who are having problems in getting along with other workers. One very new branch of psychology is *parapsychology*, which studies powers of extrasensory perception.

History of Psychology Psychology became established as a science in 1879, when Wilhelm Wundt set up the first psychological laboratory in Leipzig, Germany. Between that time and the 1930's, four different ways of studying the mind were developed. These approaches or methods are called *structuralism*, *behaviorism*, *gestalt psychology*, and *psychoanalysis*.

The structural psychologists tried to describe and analyze the way people experience or perceive things through their senses. For example, the sense of sight gives the mind a great deal of information, such as shape, color, distance, size, and so on. The sense of touch gives information about texture, heat, cold, pain, wetness, and so on. The structural psychologists wanted to find out what kinds of information the human mind was getting.

The behavioral psychologists began laboratory experiments on the way people and animals behave in various situations. The Russian scientist, Ivan Pavlov, had conducted experiments on the reflexes of dogs. Behavioral psychologists extended those experiments to find out how people or animals *usually* behave; *if* behavior can be changed; and *how* behavior can be changed.

The gestalt psychologists were interested in how people's minds are organized—how the mind sorts out information. Gestalt is a German word meaning "pattern" or "form." Gestalt psychologists believed that people perceive things in patterns or groups. For example, when you look at a tree, you perceive all at once a whole object that has a trunk, branches, leaves, roots, and so on. You do not first see leaves, then a trunk, then branches, each separately. Gestalt psychologists created tests to determine the patterns of perception that people have. The most famous of these is the inkblot test, in which a person describes the shapes and objects that he thinks he sees in the inkblot.

Psychoanalysis began around 1900 with the work of Sigmund Freud. Freud believed that persons tend to *repress* (push out of their conscious, or thinking, mind) any thoughts or memories that they or other people do not approve of. Freud said that these repressed thoughts and memories have a great effect on people's behavior. Through psychoanalysis, people could be made to remember their repressed thoughts and memories, and then be able to change their behavior and work out their mental problems.

Today, psychologists are using a variety of approaches and methods. Psychologists work in businesses and industries, and fields of advertising, public relations, and education. Hospitals, prisons, schools, and public welfare agencies employ psychologists. Maybe you will study psychology and join in the fascinating exploration of the mind.

Future psychologists usually major in psychology at a college or university while studying for a bachelor's degree. After about five years of postgraduate study they can earn a doctorate in psychology. Many take up internships in clinics during their course of study as medical students do.

For further information on
Branches of Psychology, *see* AGING, EXTRASENSORY PERCEPTION, GROWTH, INTELLIGENCE, LEARNING, MENTAL HEALTH.
Elements in the Study of Psychology, *see* ADOLESCENCE, BRAIN, CULTURE, CUSTOMS, DREAM, EMOTION, HABIT, HEALTH, HORMONE, HUMAN BODY, HYPNOSIS, MEMORY, NERVOUS SYSTEM, REASONING, SENSE ORGAN.
Psychologists, *see* FREUD, SIGMUND; JUNG, CARL; PAVLOV, IVAN.
Sciences and Other Fields Related to Psychology, *see* ANTHROPOLOGY, CHILD CARE, EDUCATION, GENETICS, GUIDANCE, MEDICINE, PHILOSOPHY, SCIENCE, SOCIAL WORK, SOCIOLOGY, SPECIAL EDUCATION, TEACHING.

PUBERTY see ADOLESCENCE.

PUBLIC HEALTH You and your schoolmates have vaccinations to keep you from getting diseases that can be spread from one person to others. You drink water without any fear that it will give you a disease. Providing health education and making water safe to drink are public health actions. Public health is the field of medicine and hygiene that deals with preventing diseases in the community.

Almost every community has a department of public health. This department is responsible for a number of things. It enforces standards of cleanliness for the handling and preparing of foods in restaurants. It tries to prevent epidemics. It makes sure that garbage and trash are taken away from homes and streets so that these wastes are not a threat to the health of the people. It gives advice to women on how to care for their health before their babies are born and how to care for their babies and small children.

The public health department keeps records on what diseases the

▼ *The danger of pollution has prompted some local authorities to warn citizens of the danger to their health from swimming in the water of some streams and rivers.*

▲ *A scene with which we are all too familiar—carelessly discarded trash at the water's edge. Legislation alone cannot control such thoughtless behavior; everyone must become more conscious of the environment.*

citizens suffer. It sets standards for the construction and care of public vehicles (buses, trains, and so on), recreation centers, beaches, and private, as well as public, buildings. The public health department made sure that when your school was built it had enough windows, good plumbing, and an adequate system for getting rid of garbage. In larger communities, public health departments have nurses who, among their other duties, visit and help old and feeble persons in their homes.

People who work in public health must have medical and scientific training. Public health workers include doctors, nurses, and those trained for special jobs, such as testing the purity of water.

The idea of public health was understood in a small way even in ancient times. Cities had laws that required garbage and other wastes to be kept out of certain parts of a city. People had some idea that there was a connection between filth and disease, but they did not know what the connection was. In the 1800's, bacteria and viruses were discovered to be the causes of diseases that can be passed from one person to another. Once this was understood, laws governing public health were passed, and doctors and other public health workers were able to help prevent the spread of diseases. In the first part of the 1900's, scientists discovered vitamins and other things necessary for a healthy diet. These discoveries made it possible for public health workers to help keep the people of a community healthier.

The Public Health Service is an agency of the Department of Health and Human Services. The Public Health Service is directed by the Surgeon General. One of its bureaus enforces quarantine laws to prevent epidemics and examines immigrants to make sure they do not have diseases others can catch. It also operates federal hospitals and clinics. Another bu-

reau helps the states, foreign governments, and organizations operate health programs. The National Institutes of Health study physical and mental diseases.

■ **LEARN BY DOING**

You can do much to contribute to public health. Stay away from others as much as you can when you have a cold or any other illness that is contagious. Cover your nose and mouth when you cough or sneeze. Keep all garbage and waste in closed containers. If you pass an uncovered garbage can on the street, cover it! Don't drink water if you are not sure it is pure. Report anything that you think is a menace to public health. ■

ALSO READ: BACTERIA, CONTAGIOUS DISEASES, IMMUNITY, VIRUS.

PUBLIC RELATIONS The art of winning people's favor for an organization or an individual is known as public relations. Many businesses (car makers, airlines, hotels, and so on) employ experts in public relations to inform the public and get it to think well of them.

To do this, public relations people try to have favorable stories about their employers published in newspa-

▼ *Queen Elizabeth II of Britain has little real power, but she does an important public relations job for her country at home and abroad.*

pers, magazines, or books. They try to use radio and television programs for the same purpose. They give free photographs of the people or places they are publicizing to newspapers and magazines. Sometimes they entertain important customers who visit the company.

Public relations and advertising are closely connected. Public relations helps to "sell" a company to the public. Advertising helps to sell the goods that company produces. Sometimes public relations and advertising work together to promote both the company and its products. For example, a sporting goods store might buy baseball shirts for a Little League team. By doing this, the store manager may hope to get good publicity for the store and also sell products to league members and others in the community.

People who use public relations firms include men and women who are candidates for election to public office. The public relations experts try to build what they call a favorable image of their client. They want to make the voters like the candidate so much that they will vote for him or her.

■ LEARN BY DOING

If a friend of yours is running for a class office, you can do public relations work for him or her. Arrange for the candidate to be interviewed by a staff member from your school or class newspaper. Find out what issues your classmates are interested in and have your candidate talk about them in speeches. ■

ALSO READ: ADVERTISING.

PUBLIC SPEAKING If you have ever made a speech to your class, you already know something about public speaking. You know that you must know your subject well in order to earn the respect of your audience.

◄ *Your first experience of public speaking will probably take place at a school gathering.*

You know that your speech must be interesting to make your audience listen to you at all! Experienced speakers are also aware that they must know their audience—their interests and their opinions.

A speech should be well organized. In the *introduction*, the speaker should attract the listeners' attention and make them want to hear the speech. In the *body* of the speech, the speaker should state the main ideas and explain them clearly. The kind of explanation depends on the requirements of the speech. Examples, facts, reasons, and comparisons are frequently used to support the main ideas. The *conclusion* should present a brief summary of what the speaker has said. The conclusion helps the audience remember the most important points of the speech.

Like all other kinds of communication, public speaking involves a message to send, a sender, and a receiver. In this case, there is a spoken message (the speech), a speaker, and listeners. Each plays an equally important part.

The public speaker stirs up ideas and feelings in the listeners in at least three ways. What the audience sees influences its opinion of the speaker and his or her message. The speaker's posture, gestures, facial expression,

There are many long speeches on record in the United States Senate. The longest continuous speech was delivered by Senator Wayne Morse in 1953. He spoke for 22 hours 26 minutes without sitting down!

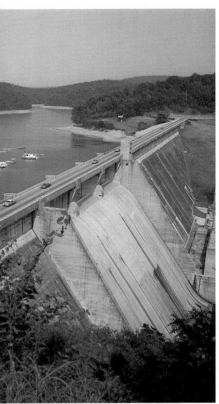

▲ *In 1933, the U.S. government set up the Tennessee Valley Authority (TVA) to control floods, improve navigation, and produce electricity in the region of the Tennessee River and its tributaries. The Norris dam, shown here, was the first dam to be built by the TVA, a public utility company.*

and body movements are all important. The way the speaker uses his or her voice can change the meaning of the speech. The loudness of sounds, their pitch (high, medium, and low), and the emphasis put on words influence the meaning of what is said. Some words have several possible meanings, and the listener can tell which meaning is intended by the way the speaker uses his or her voice. The choice of words used by the speaker also affects the way the listener will react.

Most public speeches are one of three general kinds. The speech meant *to inform* is intended to give the audience information on a particular subject. For example, if you gave a speech to your class on caring for a pet rabbit, the speech would be informative. A speech intended *to persuade* tries to convince the audience that the speaker's opinions are correct. Speeches given by politicians are persuasive speeches. The speech meant *to entertain* is amusing (if it is successful) and helps create a mood of easy enjoyment. For example, speeches given at banquets are often meant simply to entertain.

■ **LEARN BY DOING**

Write a speech (introduction, body, and conclusion) on a subject that interests you and most people in your class. Be sure to decide before you begin whether your speech is to be informative, persuasive, or entertaining. With your teacher's permission, present your speech to the class. Remember, all public speakers are nervous. ■

In a good public speech of whatever type, the speaker stimulates the audience through the speech and the way he or she presents it. The audience in turn stimulates the speaker by reacting to what is said. The speech becomes an active experience for all.

ALSO READ: PRONUNCIATION, SPEECH.

PUBLIC UTILITY When you turn on a lamp in your house, you are using a public utility. Public utilities are businesses that supply services such as light, heat, power, telephone, telegraph, water, and garbage disposal. Transportation services are also public utilities. These include delivery services, airplanes, buses, subways, and trains.

Public utilities are owned by the government in many countries. But in the United States, most public utilities are owned by private companies. The Federal Government, however, does carefully regulate the way in which some public utilities are run. The government tells public utility companies how much to charge for their services.

Some cities and towns own public utilities. Local city or town governments sometimes own airports, bus and subway systems, water supply systems, garbage disposal facilities, and sewage systems.

The Federal Government owns some of the power plants that supply electricity in the United States. The Tennessee Valley Authority is the best known of these U.S. government-owned public utilities.

A public utility company is usually

▼ *Public utility companies use high-power transmission lines, strung from tall towers, to carry electricity from generating plants.*

the only one in an area to provide a certain service. This means that the company has a *monopoly* on the service. Because public utility companies provide important services, communities depend on them. A strike at a public utility—so that garbage is not picked up or telephones don't work—can cause a community crisis. Government regulation of public utilities is therefore necessary.

ALSO READ: ELECTRIC POWER, TELE-COMMUNICATIONS, TELEGRAPH, TELE-PHONE, TENNESSEE, TRANSPORTA-TION, WATER SUPPLY.

PUBLISHING

The business of selecting, editing, printing, advertising, and distributing printed material is called publishing. Publishing companies put written words and *visuals* (pictures, photographs, charts, and diagrams) together to produce books, magazines, newspapers, pamphlets, and other types of printed material.

The publishing of printed material requires the creative talents and skills of many people. Although publishing techniques differ depending on the material being published, the general process is similar for all types of material. Let's say you have written a book and you want to have it published. First you send a typed copy of your book (called the *manuscript*) to a publishing company. Several *editors* decide whether or not to publish it.

If your book is accepted for publication, an editor works with you in revising (changing) or rewriting the manuscript, if necessary. Then the manuscript is given to a *copy editor* who prepares it for the printer. The copy editor corrects any mistakes in grammar, spelling, or punctuation, and checks to be sure all information in the manuscript is correct.

The editor and a *designer* work together to decide your book's *layout*. They determine the size of the page, the number of pages, and the design

▲ *A designer at work in a publishing house. Great skill is required in preparing pictures and text for the printer.*

of the book's cover (called the *binding*) and the book jacket, if there is to be one.

Once the layout is established, the *production* department goes to work. The production staff works directly with the printer to see that your book gets printed and bound. Your final revised manuscript is marked with directions to the printer on how to set it in type. The typesetter does a sample setting that comes back to the editor on long sheets of paper called *galleys. Proofreaders* check the galleys word for word against your original manuscript to be sure the material has been set in type correctly. An extra set of galleys is cut apart and pasted onto rough layouts of the book, with space left for the visuals. These rough layouts become a *working dummy.*

The corrected galleys and the dummy are returned to the printer to be set in final page form according to the arrangement in the dummy. *Page proofs* follow, and finally proofs with visuals in place in order to allow a last check. Then a certain number of copies of your book are printed, bound, and shipped to places where they will be sold.

Long before the final printing, plans are made for selling your book. The sales and marketing departments decide how many copies will be printed and where and how they will be sold. Promotion schemes (publi-

The first book in English published in the United States was the *Bay Psalm Book*. It was printed by Stephen Day in 1640 in Cambridge, Massachusetts.

▲ *In the publisher's art department, a designer prepares the layout of an illustrated page, indicating the position of illustrations, artwork and text for a page much like this one.*

▼ *A herd on the move in front of this Pueblo Indian settlement and church at Taos, New Mexico. The Indians' public religious ceremonies attract tourists annually.*

city and advertising) are put into action to arouse people's interest in your forthcoming book. Finally, sales persons sell your book to bookstores, which sell it to their customers.

Many types of publishing companies produce different kinds of material. *Book publishers* are of two sorts. *Trade book publishers* handle all books of general interest to the public, such as fiction, poetry, history, biographies, cooking, reference books, plus many others. *Educational publishers* handle textbooks, workbooks, and any other printed materials written to instruct students and intended to be sold to schools. Some publishers handle both trade and educational books.

Magazine publishing is divided into general-interest *mass magazines*, and *special-interest magazines* (such as scientific journals, hobby magazines, and so on). *Newspaper publishing* involves the production of printed news. Newspapers are divided into categories according to size of readership and frequency of circulation (whether they are published daily, weekly, or monthly). Some newspapers specialize in certain kinds of material, such as local community news.

■ LEARN BY DOING

If you should become interested in working in the publishing industry, there is a wide variety of jobs available—writing, editing, proofreading, photography, art, designing, typesetting, printing, advertising, marketing, selling, and many others. You can begin right now getting experience by working on a school newspaper or magazine. If your school does not have one, why not start one! ■

ALSO READ: ADVERTISING, BOOK, COMMUNICATION, DESIGN, JOURNALISM, MAGAZINE, NEWSPAPER, PHOTOGRAPHY, PRINTING, TYPESETTING.

PUEBLO INDIANS The Pueblo Indians are a group of closely related Indian tribes that live in New Mexico and Arizona. When Spanish explorers arrived in New Mexico in the early 1500's, they found Indians living there in villages built of *adobe* (sun-dried mud and straw) brick. The Spaniards named them Pueblo Indians, because the word *pueblo* means "village" in Spanish.

The ancestors of the Pueblo Indians were the first people to inhabit the Southwest. They were farmers who grew corn, beans, and cotton. They wove cloth from the cotton and made baskets and pottery. They also hunted for small game. The Pueblo Indians were shorter and darker than their neighbors, the Indians who lived in the Great Plains.

The lives of Pueblo Indians today reflect the ways of their ancestors. They still live in adobe homes and work as farmers. But the Spanish taught them to raise sheep and cattle, and they no longer hunt. Pottery-making has become a highly developed art. The two main tribes of Pueblo Indians are the Hopi and the Zuñi.

The Pueblo Indians worship a number of nature gods. The "Snake Dance" was one of their most important religious ceremonies. Dancers carried live rattlesnakes in their mouths as a kind of prayer for rain.

ALSO READ: CLIFF DWELLERS; INDIAN ART, AMERICAN; INDIANS, AMERICAN.

PUERTO RICO

Capital City: San Juan (429,000 people).
Area: 3,421 square miles (8,860 sq. km).
Population: 3,286,000.
Government: Commonwealth—self governing part of United States.
Export Products: Tobacco, sugar, and molasses.
Unit of Money: U.S. dollar.
Official Languages: Spanish and English.

ATLANTIC OCEAN
El Yunque Rain Forest
Arecibo
San Juan
Culebra I.
Mayagüez
Caguas
Ponce
Vieques I.
Cerro de Puntas (4,389 ft.)
CARIBBEAN SEA
PLAINS
HIGHLANDS
MOUNTAINS

PUERTO RICO The Common-wealth of Puerto Rico is an island in the West Indies with more than three million inhabitants. Its capital and largest city is the beautiful port city of San Juan. The Caribbean Sea lies to the south of Puerto Rico and the Atlantic Ocean is on the north. The island lies about 885 miles (1,425 km) southeast of Florida. Puerto Rico is a commonwealth that governs itself, but it has the military protection and certain economic and political privi-leges of the United States. Puerto Ricans are U.S. citizens, but they cannot vote for President or members of Congress.

Puerto Rican cities are situated in the coastal lowlands. Farmland is in the nearby valleys. Mountains rise in the south central part of the island. The rain forest on the slopes of the mountain El Yunque, not far from San Juan, sometimes has as much as 200 inches (500 cm) of rainfall a year. Huge tropical trees and exotic flowers grow wild there.

Many Puerto Ricans make their living by farming, although manufac-turing provides more jobs. Sugar-cane, coconuts, pineapples and other fruits, and tobacco are some of the main crops. Livestock and dairy products are important to the econo-my. Puerto Ricans are largely of Spanish descent and most of them speak Spanish at home. Education is mainly in Spanish, although English is taught from the first grade on.

Christopher Columbus discovered Puerto Rico in 1493. The explorer, Ponce de León, claimed the island for Spain in 1509 and started a Spanish settlement. Carib and Arawak Indi-ans were living on the island then. Its rich vegetation and reports of gold made the Spanish call the island Puerto Rico, the "rich port." The gold soon gave out, however, and the island beame a Spanish colony of large plantations. Black slaves brought by the Spaniards from Africa during the 1700's and 1800's were the ancestors of some Puerto Ricans. El Morro, a fortress built by the Span-iards at the Bay of San Juan, still stands. In 1898, Spain granted the island self-rule. Soon after, it was occupied by U.S. troops during the Spanish-American War and given by Spain to the United States.

U.S. citizens soon acquired most of the major plantations, and many Puerto Ricans became restless with what they considered to be second-class status. In 1917, however, the Jones Act passed by the U.S. Con-gress gave full citizenship to Puerto Ricans and allowed them some self-rule. In 1947, they were allowed to choose their own governor. These moves did not satisfy the Nationalist Party of the country, which led an unsuccessful revolution in 1950. The United States decided to allow the island to draft its own constitution. Puerto Ricans then were allowed to

Children in Puerto Rico celebrate "Three Kings Day" on January 6, at the end of the Christmas season. They receive gifts on this day as well as on Christmas Day.

▲ *Puerto Rico's sandy beaches and sunny climate make the island a popular vacation spot for tourists from the mainland of the United States.*

choose among complete independence, full statehood within the United States, or a continuation of commonwealth status. A majority of the voters chose to remain a commonwealth. Puerto Ricans elect their governor and a legislative assembly.

Puerto Rico is a densely populated island. More than a third of the people live in the six largest cities—Bayamón, Caguas, Carolina, Mayagüez, Ponce, and San Juan. Overpopulation and high unemployment caused thousands of Puerto Ricans to emigrate to the United States in the 1950's and 1960's. Since about 1975, the island's economy has markedly improved, and Puerto Ricans have found more jobs. "Operation Bootstrap," an economic plan of the Puerto Rican government, encouraged large-scale U.S. investment. The government helped factory owners find locations and train workers. Thousands of people are employed in factories that make textiles, chemicals, electrical equipment, and many other products. Other factories process food and refine sugar.

The tropical climate and sandy beaches attract many tourists to Puerto Rico. Big hotels have been built in the Condado Beach section of San Juan and in other parts of the island.

ALSO READ: COLUMBUS, CHRISTOPHER; SPANISH-AMERICAN WAR.

▶ *Three common types of pumps: (A) reciprocating or displacement pump, (B) rotary pump, and (C) centrifugal pump.*

PULSAR see STAR.

PULSE see CIRCULATORY SYSTEM.

PUMA see CAT, WILD.

PUMP A pump is a machine that moves a fluid (a liquid or a gas). A bicycle pump is a kind of pump. So is an electric fan.

A *reciprocating*, or *displacement*, pump works by sucking or pulling fluid into a chamber through an *intake* opening and then pushing it out of the chamber through an *outlet* opening. When you pull up on the handle of a bicycle pump, a piston inside the pump moves up and air from outside rushes in through an intake valve (an opening with a lid on it). When you

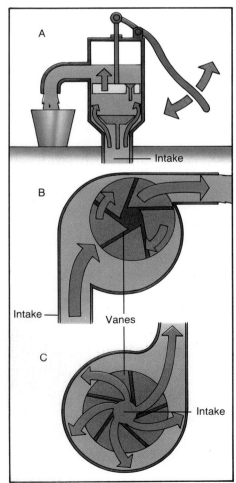

press down on the handle, the piston forces the air out through an outlet valve into the bicycle tire. The lids of the two valves open in different directions, so that the air pressure that forces one valve open forces the other valve shut. This makes sure that the air only comes in the intake valve and only goes out the outlet valve.

A *rotary* pump is a kind of displacement pump that doesn't have a piston. Instead, it has a wheel that turns inside. The wheel uncovers the intake and sucks the fluid in. Then it closes the intake and uncovers the outlet and forces the fluid out. Gasoline pumps are rotary pumps. Some rotary pumps have gears inside. The gears catch the fluid from the intake between their teeth and carry it around to the outlet. Gear pumps are very strong. They are used to pump thick liquids, such as oil.

In an *axial flow* pump, such as an electric fan, the air comes in the back and is picked up by blades that force it out the front.

In a *centrifugal* pump, the fluid comes in through an intake in the middle and is picked up by flat blades that whip it around to the outside and force it through the outlet. Imagine a fan with the blades bent so that air is forced from the inside of the fan out, instead of from front to back. This will give you an idea of how a centrifugal pump works.

■ LEARN BY DOING

There are many other kinds of pumps. Pumps are useful and important. How many pumps are there in your home? In an automobile? Are there any pumps in your body? ■

ALSO READ: PHYSICS.

PUNCTUATION As you listen to your friends talk, you will notice that their speech is full of little pauses and changes in *pitch* (high, low, or in-between sounds). These pauses and pitch changes help you understand more easily what your friends are saying. Punctuation marks are the symbols used in written language to indicate the little pauses and changes of pitch that would be heard if you were speaking the words aloud.

Hyphen ▬ A hyphen is a mark used either as a connector or a separator. In some cases, hyphens connect the words to suggest a continuous sound, such as "clang-clang-clang." The hyphen is also used in connecting two different words to create a new meaning.

Example: Spanish-speaking.

The hyphen is used at the end of a line to divide a word that is to be continued on the next line.

Example: It will be better to arrive at suppertime.

Period . A period is a full-stop punctuation mark. In written language, a period is placed where the sound of the voice would stop if the sentence were spoken aloud. In sentences asking questions or expressing deep emotion, other marks are added to the period, making ? (for a question) and ! (for an exclamation).

Semicolon ; Another full-stop mark is the semicolon. It marks a logical break in the progress of a sentence. It is often used to connect the two main clauses of a compound sentence when a conjunction, such as "and," is not used. (I couldn't sleep; I woke up at midnight.) When a conjunction is used between the main clauses, a semicolon is used if the main clauses contain commas. Semicolons are also used to separate items in a series when the items are very long or when other punctuation, such as a comma, is used within the items.

Example: On our trip west, we stopped at Portland, Eugene, and Myrtle Point in Oregon; Crescent City, Eureka, and Sausalito in California; and Phoenix in Arizona.

▲ *This windmill powers a water pump used on a farm.*

No one knows when puppets were first used as a form of entertainment. Ancient Greek literature of 300 B.C. refers to "string-pullers"—puppeteers.

▲ *Kermit the frog, one of the Muppets, popular TV and movie puppets.*

Apostrophe ' An apostrophe and the letter "s" are usually added to a noun when ownership (possession) is shown, as in "the city's night noises." When a plural noun ends in "s," only the apostrophe is necessary to show possession. The apostrophe is also the mark used when joining two words together in a contraction.

Example: I + am = I'm

Quotation Marks " " When indicating exactly what someone said, or when quoting from something that has been written, quotation marks are used at the beginning and again at the end of the quotation. When someone is being quoted within the quotation, single quotation marks (") are used.

Example: Anne said, "He told me, 'I left it in the desk drawer.' "

Exclamation Point ! The exclamation point is used to express emotion or show emphasis.

Example: Look out!

Comma , The comma makes reading easier, just as the pause for breath makes speaking easier. As a punctuation mark, the comma indicates a brief pause in the flow of a sentence or some portion of it. Commas are also used to separate the items of a series when the items themselves do not contain commas.

Example: When you get a flat tire, it helps to have a spare, a jack, a lug wrench, and someone to change the tire for you.

Question Mark ? Sometimes called "the interrogation point," the question mark is used at the end of any material phrased as a question. Otherwise, the meaning would be different.

Examples: You'll meet me at five? You'll meet me at five.

Colon : The colon usually indicates a longer pause than the comma and semicolon. It is often used before a list of items. It shows that what follows is connected to some degree with what went before. Colons are also used after the salutation of a business letter (Dear Ms. Jones:) and in writing the time (2:30).

Parentheses ( ) Parentheses indicate an interruption and set off additional material or an explanation that is helpful but not really necessary to the meaning of the sentence.

Example: The chairs (but not the tables) can be moved easily.

Dash —— The function of a single dash is somewhat like that of the comma or colon. A pair of dashes is used in the same way that parentheses are used.

Example: John—who teaches physical education—is the Little League coach.

Punctuation serves written language in many useful ways. For more details on the functions of each kind of punctuation mark, consult a grammar textbook or the special section on punctuation in a dictionary.

ALSO READ: GRAMMAR, PARTS OF SPEECH.

PUPPET The word "puppet" comes from the Latin word *pupa*, meaning "doll." A puppet is a doll that is made to move. You have probably seen puppets on television, such as the "Muppets" of *Sesame Street*. In the past, children enjoyed the television puppet performances on the *Howdy Doody* and the *Kukla, Fran, and Ollie* shows.

There are six basic kinds of puppets. A *hand puppet* is worn over the hand, like a mitten. The forefinger is placed in the neck to operate the head. The thumb and middle finger operate the arms. A person, called a *puppeteer*, works the hand puppet from a position behind and below the stage.

A *rod* or *stick puppet* is also operated from beneath the stage. With one hand, the puppeteer holds the puppet's body upright with a rod. With the other hand, he or she moves rods attached to the puppet's arms and head. The rods are in back of the puppet and cannot be seen by the audience unless the puppet is accidentally turned around.

Shadow puppets are actually rod puppets. Instead of watching the puppets directly, the audience watches a screen on which the puppets' shadows are cast. Some shadow puppets are made of colorful, translucent materials, such as glass or plastic. The light shines through these materials so that color as well as shape can be seen on the screen. Shadow puppets can be turned in almost any direction, because the audience never sees the rods that work them.

To operate *finger puppets*, the puppeteer's middle finger and forefinger become the puppet's legs. Tiny shoes are worn on the fingertips, and the puppet's upper body is strapped to the top of the puppeteer's hand. With the free hand, the puppeteer uses strings to operate the head and arms. When working a finger puppet, the puppeteer's hand must be on stage. The puppeteer usually wears black, long-sleeved clothing during a performance so his or her presence will not be so noticeable.

A ventriloquist is someone who has learned to speak without moving the lips. He or she holds a *dummy* (a large doll) on the knee, placing one hand in the dummy's back to operate the head, eyes, mouth, and arms. During a performance, the ventriloquist, without moving his or her own lips, makes the dummy move and speak so that it seems as if the dummy were talking. One of the most famous ventriloquists was Edgar Bergen whose dummy was a fast-talking wise guy, Charlie MacCarthy.

Marionettes are string-operated puppets. The puppeteer stands above and behind the stage, controlling the marionette with as many as 30 strings. Simpler marionettes are made with seven strings running to the hands, knees, sides of the head, and back of the puppet.

Recently, an electrically operated, remote-control puppet has been invented. This kind of puppet is able to move around a stage without the aid of strings or a puppeteer's hand. The puppet's body is made of soft materials that allow the puppeteer to control its movements.

No one knows exactly where or when puppets originated. The ancient Hindus of India believed that puppets were friends of gods. Ancient Egyptians had puppets, representing spirits and gods, which were carried in religious processions. Puppet plays were a favorite form of entertainment in ancient China, Japan, Greece, Rome, and Indonesia.

During the Middle Ages, Italian puppeteers gave performances throughout Europe. Puppet plays were presented on tiny stages set up in buildings or on street corners. Most early European puppet plays were based on religious or Biblical stories. During the 1300's and 1400's, fables and comedies became popular. One of the favorite puppet characters of those days was *Pulcinella*, who was portrayed as a flirt and prankster. In France, Pulcinella became *Polichinelle*, and in Spain became known as *Don Cristobal Pulchin-*

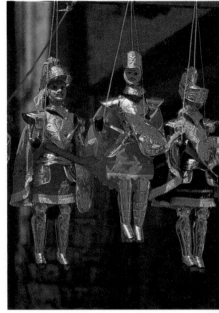

▲ *These colorful armored soldier-puppets are hanging up for sale in a souvenir store on the island of Sicily.*

▼ *Street puppet shows are performed in many cities of the world. They are always sure to attract a large audience of young people.*

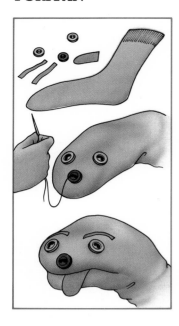

ela. The French Polichinelle was taken to England in 1662, where he became known as *Punch.* English puppeteers gave Punch a wife named Judy. The famous "Punch and Judy Shows" have amused audiences in Europe and the United States for many years. In Italy and other countries, Pinocchio (a puppet who turns into a boy) became another favorite character. A favorite German puppet was Hans Wurst (John Sausage), and in the Netherlands Jan Pickel Herringe (John Pickled Herring) was a popular puppet character.

Puppetry is a form of drama, and in many areas of the world it has developed into a great art. In Asia, puppeteers have created elaborate, complicated puppets that wear beautifully decorated costumes. In China and Indonesia, shadow plays (in which puppets are operated behind lighted curtains) have been popular for centuries. Puppeteers from all over the world come to train at the Central State Puppet Theater in Moscow in the Soviet Union. The Teatro del Nahuatl in Mexico City is another of the world's great puppet theaters.

■ LEARN BY DOING

You can make a hand puppet of your own, using an old sock. Put your hand into the sock. Decide where you want the eyes and nose, and sew buttons on for each. Yarn or scraps of material can be glued or sewn on to make hair, eyebrows, a beard, costumes, or any other kind of decoration. Sock puppets also make good animal characters.

In front of a mirror, practice making the puppet show different emotions—anger, sadness, joy, fear, and surprise—by changing the positions of the puppet's body. Try out various facial expressions by moving your fingers around in the sock. Then give your puppet a voice and practice making the puppet's actions fit the words. ■

ALSO READ: ACTORS AND ACTING, DOLL, DRAMA.

PURITAN Many Protestants in England about 400 years ago were known as Puritans because they wished to "purify" the services of the Church of England. Puritans wanted to do away with elaborate rituals or ceremonies. All English people, however, were expected to worship God in the manner decided by the king and church authorities. Puritans who refused were severely punished. Many felt it was dangerous to remain in their native land, and they decided to seek freedom in America.

In 1629, a group of Puritans formed the Massachusetts Bay Company. The king gave them a charter granting them permission to settle on land not far from Plymouth, a town founded by the Pilgrims in 1620. The Puritans landed in the New World and named their settlement Boston.

During the next few years, other Puritans crossed the Atlantic and started other towns. The people who settled all important matters in the colony had to be members of the Puritan church, and anyone who disagreed with them ran the risk of harsh punishment. The Puritans used punishments such as *stocks,* a wood frame with holes for confining the ankles, wrists, and sometimes the head. (The person being punished would be put in stocks in a public place to shame him or her.) The Puritans had come to the New World to find religious freedom, but they were not willing to give the same freedom to others.

Many Puritans who wanted real religious freedom left and started new settlements. Roger Williams founded what is now Rhode Island, and Thomas Hooker founded what is now Connecticut.

Puritans who remained in England supported the civil war that started in 1642 and ended with the beheading of King Charles I in 1649. (These Puritans were called Roundheads because they cut their hair short.) They established a commonwealth led by Oliver

▼ *The* Mayflower *sets out in 1620 for America, carrying the group of Puritans who left England to find religious freedom in the New World.*

Cromwell in 1649. After disagreements within the government, the commonwealth was ended. A Protectorate was established with Cromwell as the absolute ruler. The Puritan government was tolerant of most Protestant religions but no others. It forced a very strict morality on English life. In 1660, the monarchy was reestablished. The Puritans were then treated even more harshly than they had been before the revolution. Many years passed before Puritans in England gained full religious freedom and all their civil rights.

ALSO READ: CONNECTICUT; CROMWELL, OLIVER; ENGLISH HISTORY; MASSACHUSETTS; PILGRIM SETTLERS; RHODE ISLAND; WILLIAMS, ROGER.

PYGMY   A Pygmy, or Pigmy, is a member of any of several short peoples who live in parts of Africa and Asia. The word "pygmy" refers generally to someone or something small. Pygmies range from 4 to 5 feet (1.2 to 1.5 m) in height. They have a lighter skin color than many black people have. Some anthropologists (scientists who study human cultures) consider the Pygmies part of the Negroid race, but others believe they are a separate race. Pygmies are a friendly, peaceful people.

African Pygmies, sometimes called *Negrillos,* live in the dense, tropical jungles and rain forests of Burundi, Cameroon, Congo, Gabon, Rwanda, and Zaire. African Pygmies live in groups of about 20 families. They hunt and gather honey, fruit, and vegetables. They use nets to trap animals and then kill them with spears or bows and arrows, often poison-tipped. This method enables Pygmies to kill even very large animals, such as antelopes and buffaloes. Pygmies migrate (move) often from place to place within the jungle in search of fresh game. They live in huts made of twigs and leaves. Pygmies trade with Afri-

can villagers who live near them.

Asian Pygmies, sometimes called *Negritos,* live in southeastern Asia, mainly on the Malay Peninsula and the Philippine and Andaman islands. Their skin color may range from yellow to black (African Pygmies usually have a reddish-brown skin), and their hair may be thick and long (African Pygmies usually have short, curly hair). Asian Pygmies have a life similar to that of the African Pygmies, but some of them now live permanently in one place and farm or work as laborers.

Most Pygmy populations are declining because of interbreeding with other groups, low birth rates, and high infant death rates. Pygmies may possibly become extinct in the future.

ALSO READ: AFRICA, GROWTH, JUNGLE, PACIFIC ISLANDS.

PYRAMID   In geometry, a pyramid is a solid shape with a many-sided base and triangular sides sloping up to a point. In architecture, a pyramid is a large structure with the same shape. Most of these pyramids are made of stone and have a square base and four sides. Sometimes the sides are stepped.

Pyramids have been built in many parts of the world. The most famous pyramids are those of ancient Egypt. About 4,500 years ago, an Egyptian pharaoh (king) named Zoser ordered the first pyramid built as a burial tomb. Until that time, most Egyptians had built small mudbrick tombs called *mastabas.* Zoser's Step Pyramid at Saqqara (near Cairo) was the world's first all-stone structure. It was called a "step pyramid" because it rose in levels like huge stepping stones. Cheops, Khafre, and Menkaure, later pharaohs, built three massive pyramids at Giza. Cheops' Great Pyramid was the first of these. It took about 20 years to complete. It was originally 481 feet (147 m) high,

▲ *A pygmy of the Bambuti tribe that lives in the forests of Zaire.*

The Great Pyramid of Cheops took 200,000 slaves 20 years to build. They used over 2,500,000 stone blocks. The positioning of the blocks is so exact that on some facing stones it is still impossible to insert a piece of paper in the joints. The fact that this massive structure is still standing after 4,500 years is proof indeed of the ancient Egyptians' engineering skills.

▲ *The great pyramids at Giza in Egypt are an awesome achievement, even judged by today's advanced engineering methods.*

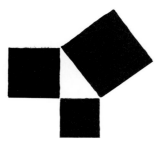

▲ *The Pythagorean theorem states that the square of the longest side of a right-angled triangle equals the sum of the squares of the other two sides.*

and its base covered over 13 acres (5.3 hectares). It was made of over two million stone blocks. They weighed from 2 to 15 tons (1.8 to 13.6 metric tons) each.

About 4,000 persons worked on the project at one time. They hauled the great stone blocks up dirt ramps to the level on which they were working. When that level was finished, they built a higher ramp and started on the next level. When the top was reached, some of the stones were evened off. Facing stones were carefully added to fill in the spaces. When it was completed, the pyramid looked like a solid piece of stone. Today, many of the facing stones have disappeared, and the sides of the pyramids look as if they are covered with huge stone steps. Inside the pyramids were the pharaoh's burial chamber and many other rooms filled with marvelous treasures for a dead pharaoh's soul to use in the next life. After the burial the entrances to these chambers were sealed with huge stones. But most pyramids were later broken

into and robbed of their treasure. The ruins of about 80 pyramids remain today in Egypt.

Indians of Central America and Mexico also built great stepped temples that were like pyramids. These pyramids often had flat terraces cut into their sides, and flat tops on which temples were built. The Pyramid of the Sun at Teotihuacán near Mexico City has a larger base than any Egyptian pyramid.

ALSO READ: EGYPT, ANCIENT.

PYTHAGORAS (about 570–500 B.C.) Very little is known about the life of this great Greek thinker. He is said to have traveled in Egypt and the Far East. We know that he moved from the island of Samos, in the Mediterranean Sea, to Croton, Italy, in 529 B.C. At Croton, he founded a cult that was part scientific, part religious. He thought he was a demigod (half-god, half-human).

Pythagoras's most important ideas were about geometry and about sound. His best-known work in geometry has come down to us as the *Pythagorean Theorem*. It states that the square of the hypotenuse (long side) of a right triangle is equal to the sum of the squares of the other two sides (see the diagram on this page).

In the field of music, Pythagoras observed that the string of a musical instrument vibrates to produce a sound. He noticed that a string of half the length, but at the same tension (tautness), produces a note an octave higher. He found other simple fractions of the string's length produced musical harmonies.

He and his followers believed that numbers and music were the most important things in the universe. They thought, for example, that the planets made music as they moved.

ALSO READ: GEOMETRY, MUSIC, SOUND.

QATAR   see ARABIA.

QUAKERS   see SOCIETY OF FRIENDS.

QUANTUM   When you look at the light coming from an electric light bulb, it seems to be steady and unwavering. Actually, light is not as steady as it seems. It is given off in a vast number of tiny packages of energy, like the bullets from a machine gun. Each of these packages is called a quantum (plural: quanta). The quantum is the smallest amount of energy there is. You cannot have part of a quantum.

We think of light and other forms of energy such as radio waves and X rays as traveling in regular waves. The height of the waves depends on the brightness of the light. The color of the light depends on the distance between the waves.

Light can also be thought of as a stream of tiny quanta or *photons*. The energy of each photon depends on the wavelength and therefore the color of the light. A photon of white light has more energy than a photon of red light. This explains why a poker glows first red, then yellow, and finally white when heated in a fire. As it gets hotter, it takes in more energy and gives out waves of greater energy.

Scientists today combine the two ways of thinking about light. They think of light streaming out in packets of waves, each packet being a quantum or photon. They also think that moving particles such as electrons behave like waves as well as behaving like solid particles.

ALSO READ: ATOM; EINSTEIN, ALBERT; PHYSICS; PLANCK, MAX; SPECTRUM.

▲ *German physicist Max Planck (1858–1947) proposed and developed the quantum theory of radiation. He was awarded the 1918 Nobel Prize for physics.*

QUARRYING   Quarrying is the mining of rock or stone from large open pits, or *quarries*. As large amounts of stone are removed from the earth, the deep hole that is made is called the quarry. Marble, slate, granite, and limestone are the chief

The largest modern quarry is Bingham Canyon Copper Mine in Utah. It covers 2.8 square miles (7.2 sq. km) and is 2,500 feet (760 m) deep.

▲ *Marble, used by sculptors and for building work, is quarried by hand. Then it is polished to bring out its beautiful colors.*

One of the world's largest meteor craters lies between Hudson and Ungave bays in Quebec. Called Le Cratere du Nouveau-Quebec or the Chubb Crater, it is 2 miles (over 3 km) in diameter and 1,350 feet (400 m) deep.

kinds of rock that are quarried.

Egg-sized pieces of rock called *trap*, or *traprock*, are used as foundations on which to build highways and railroads. To quarry rocks of this size, *blasting* is used. Holes are drilled into the rock, and sticks of dynamite are put into the holes. The exploding dynamite shatters the rock into small pieces. The blasted pieces are scooped up and sorted for size. Those that are too big are put into crushing machines that break them into smaller pieces.

Building stones are used for large buildings and the foundations of bridges. These stones are quarried in large unbroken blocks or slabs. One way to cut blocks of stone is to drill a row of holes in the rock and insert special wedges into the holes. Workers hammer on the whole row of wedges at the same time. This splits off a slab of rock. Sometimes explosives are used to loosen the stone.

Channeling machines and *wire saws* are used to quarry soft stones, such as limestone and sandstone. A channeling machine looks somewhat like a small locomotive. It moves along a track. Attached to the side of the channeling machine are long chisels or very tough saws. Both are moved by steam power. The channeling machine cuts long, vertical channels deep into the stone. Then, a *gadding machine*, similar to a channeling machine, cuts a horizontal channel. This frees the block of stone. A wire saw has an endless, tough, steel wire revolving on two pulleys at the ends of a steel shaft. An *abrasive*, a gritty substance such as sand, is poured on the wire as it runs. The wire rubs across the rock and cuts it. When all the useful stone has been taken out, quarries are abandoned. Abandoned quarries often fill up with water and become deep pools. Because of their great depth, such pools are dangerous places to swim in.

ALSO READ: GRANITE, MINES AND MINING, ROCK.

QUASAR see RADIO ASTRONOMY.

QUEBEC Quebec is Canada's largest province and the one where many people speak French. Its area is slightly larger than that of Alaska, and its population is more than a fourth of the Canadian total. Ontario and Hudson Bay border Quebec on the west, and Newfoundland-Labrador on the east. New Brunswick and some of the northeastern United States are to the south. The St. Lawrence River flows through southeastern Quebec.

The Land and Climate Except for the broad, fertile lowlands beside the St. Lawrence River, Quebec is largely a hilly province, two-thirds covered with forests and dotted with thousands of lakes and white-water rivers. The Laurentian Mountains, or the

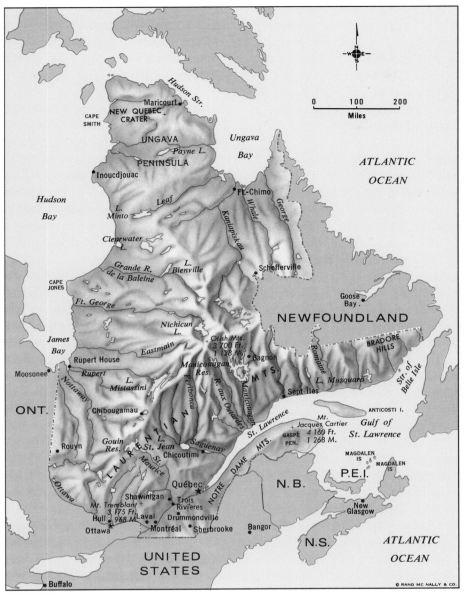

QUEBEC

Capital
Quebec City
(603,000 people)

Area
594,860 square miles
(1,540,568 sq. km)

Population
6,540,276 people

Entry into Confederation
July 1, 1867

Principal river
St. Lawrence

Highest point
Mt. Jacques Cartier
4,160 feet (1,268 m)

Largest city
Montreal (2,866,000
people in urban area).
Largest Canadian city

Famous people
William Shatner, Pierre
Trudeau

Provincial flower

Fleur de Lys

◀ *A view of the city of Quebec from the St. Lawrence River.*

▲ *Boats in the harbor of a fishing village in Quebec. Forests such as those in the background supply lumber for paper mills all over North America.*

Laurentides, are in southern Quebec.

The climate ranges from Arctic temperatures in the far northern Ungava Peninsula to more moderate temperatures in the south. Most areas have a snowfall of more than 100 inches (250 cm) a year with snow on the ground from November to April.

History   Various Indian tribes, such as the Micmac, Naskapi, and Algonquian, lived in the Quebec area when the French explorer, Jacques Cartier, landed on the Gaspé Peninsula in 1534 and claimed the area for France. Another French explorer, Samuel de Champlain, established a settlement on the site of present-day Quebec City in 1608. The area became known as New France. After the British general, James Wolfe, captured Quebec City in 1759, the area became a British colony. The Quebec Act of 1774 tried to unite the British and French in the colony. The French retained their language, religion, and customs. Quebec became known as Lower Canada in 1791. In 1867, Quebec joined three other colonies to form the new nation of Canada.

English-speaking merchants and manufacturers soon took over financial control of the province. French-Canadians centered their lives around their local churches and favored a farming and fishing way of life. The schools provided French-Canadians almost no training for business or industry. Then, in the 1960's, a "quiet revolution" began to take place in Quebec. Education was modernized and made compulsory. The provincial government started development projects.

French-Canadians demanded that French become the language of business and industry in their province. Many of them wanted Quebec to secede (withdraw) from Canada and form a separate nation. The Parti Québécois, a separatist political party, was formed in 1968. French became the province's official language

in 1974, and the Parti Québécois gained control of Quebec's legislature in 1976. Montreal is today the second largest French-speaking city in the world.

Industry   Quebec is Canada's leading supplier of iron and asbestos and is a good source of copper, zinc, and gold. The waterpower resources of the province are being harnessed by such projects as the Shipshaw hydroelectric plant on the Saguenay River. Forests supply much of the newsprint and wood products used in Canada and the United States.

Visitors to the city of Quebec will see the only "walled city" in North America. Divided into an upper and lower town, the upper town is surrounded by heavy walls built by the British in the 1800's. North of Montreal are the Laurentian ski resorts. Mont Tremblant Park and Laurentides Park are two recreation areas.

ALSO READ: CANADA, MONTREAL, ST. LAWRENCE SEAWAY.

QUICKSAND   Quicksand is a loose mass of sand that is very wet and behaves like a liquid. The more water it contains, the less weight it can carry and objects will sink into it. However, stories of people being swallowed up by quicksand are probably exaggerated. Water and sand together will support more weight than water alone, and if a person who fell into quicksand kept still it is unlikely that he or she would sink completely.

Quicksands can form in places where water is prevented from draining away from loose sand. This can happen near the mouths of large rivers, where springs rise up into sand. Quicksands are smaller and much less widespread than is often supposed. They are, however, a definite hazard in some areas.

ALSO READ: GEOLOGY, SAND.

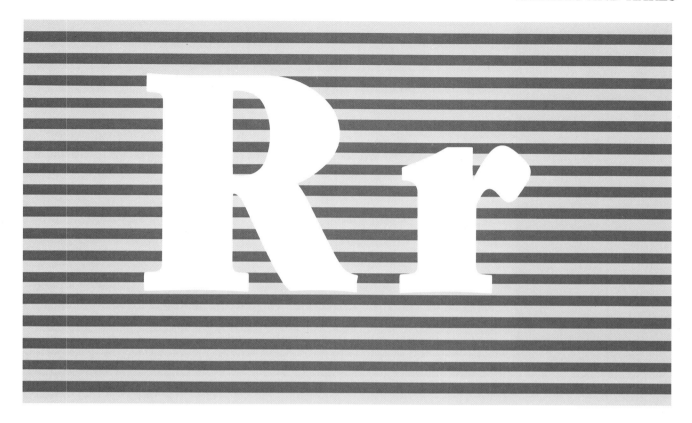

RABBITS AND HARES   It is easy to confuse rabbits and hares. The two animals are alike in many ways. Both have long ears and stubby tails. Both are good jumpers. Both are mammals. But the hare has longer ears and longer hind legs than the rabbit. Hares like to live alone, while two or three rabbit families may live together. Also, rabbits like to live underground in large burrows. Hares like to live above ground, although a hare might hide in another animal's burrow.

Both rabbits and hares are shy, timid creatures. They are the prey (hunted victims) of many animals, including human beings. Hares and rabbits are always on watch for their enemies. Their eyes let them see what is going on behind and above them.

Rabbits and hares have sharp front teeth for biting into and gnawing on vegetables. They also have flat, ridged back teeth that grind up tough plant material. The teeth keep growing throughout the animals' lives but are constantly worn down by use.

Hares   The hare we know best in the United States is called the jackrabbit. It can grow up to 25 inches (65 cm) long and weighs from 8 to 10 pounds (3.5 to 4.5 kg). The jackrabbit lives in the Midwest and West. It can run as fast as 45 miles (72 km) an hour to escape its enemies. It can even swim across rivers. The jackrabbit hides most of the day under bushes. It comes out only at night to eat grass, but it will eat any kind of vegetable or grain it can find. It especially likes

▼ *The mountain hare has two coats—one for summer, one for winter—to camouflage it against its surroundings.*

Summer coat

Winter coat

Mountain hare

▲ *The common rabbit, snug in its grassy burrow.*

▼ *Young rabbits grazing; they usually stay close to the burrow and keep the grass there very short.*

garden vegetables and corn. The jackrabbit can be a great pest to farmers.

A male jackrabbit is called a buck. A female is called a doe. The doe can have babies about four times a year. She may have as many as four at a time. The young are born with full coats of hair and with their eyes open. The doe feeds her children for about two weeks. She then leaves the young jackrabbits to take care of themselves.

Rabbits Like the hare, the rabbit comes out to eat at night. It also eats vegetables and grain. The rabbit is always on the lookout for danger. If it sees any enemies about, it thumps a hind leg hard against the ground. The noise warns other rabbits.

The cottontail rabbit is commonly found in the eastern part of the United States. It is usually about 16 to 17 inches (40 to 43 cm) long and weighs about 3 pounds (1.4 kg).

A female cottontail has babies up to eight times a year. The mother may have as many as ten at a time. The doe has her young in a special nest she builds in the ground. The young rabbits are born blind and without any fur on their bodies. When they are about three weeks old, they are old enough to take care of themselves.

Rabbits make gentle, affectionate pets. They are clean and easy to care for and are happy indoors or out.

ALSO READ: ANIMAL, ANIMAL DEFENSES, ANIMAL DISTRIBUTION, ANIMAL HOMES, ANIMAL TRACKS, MAMMAL, PET.

RABIES Rabies is a virus disease. It attacks the nervous system of warm-blooded animals, including human beings. The virus can be passed from one animal to another in saliva. This is usually done through a bite by the infected animal. An animal or a human being infected with rabies will die, unless prompt medical treatment is given.

If you are ever attacked and bitten by a dog or a cat that is frothing at the mouth, or if you are bitten by a wild animal, such as a squirrel, bat, skunk, raccoon, or rabbit, you must act quickly. Call a doctor and the police. Try to keep an eye on the animal that bit you so that the police or dogcatcher can capture it. If caught, the animal will be tested to find out whether it has rabies. This is done to find out whether you must be given injections of rabies vaccine so you won't get the disease.

Rabies is also called *hydrophobia*, which means "fear of water." This

▼ *This dog shows the characteristic signs of rabies—it is baring its teeth and foaming at the mouth.*

name was given because animals infected with rabies have swollen throat muscles that contract painfully when the thirsty, infected animal tries to drink water.

ALSO READ: PASTEUR, LOUIS; VETERINARY MEDICINE; VIRUS.

RACCOON The raccoon is one of the easiest animals to recognize. It looks as if it is wearing a mask across its eyes, and its furry tail has rings around it. The raccoon lives in the woods of the United States and Canada. It likes to live near water because it can swim as well as it can climb trees. The raccoon usually sleeps all day long in the hollow of a tree. It comes out at night to eat.

Raccoons eat fruits, nuts, roots, chickens, mice and other small forest animals, fish, and even snakes. They are "fishers" by instinct. This is why a caged raccoon will often dip dry food in its water bowl before eating it.

A mother raccoon has babies about once every year. Usually the mother has four babies at a time. The young stay with their mother until they are a year old. Then they can hunt food for themselves. Northern raccoons are *partial hibernators*—that is, they go to sleep for long periods in the winter and may wake up on warm winter days and search for food. Raccoons usually live from 10 to 15 years.

■ **LEARN BY DOING**

If you are a patient and careful observer, you may be able to track a raccoon. The best place to start is on the banks of a forest pond. There you may see the tiny five-toed footprints of the raccoon on the damp ground. See if you can follow the footprints to find raccoon trails, homes, and hiding places. ■

ALSO READ: ANIMAL DISTRIBUTION, ANIMAL HOMES, ANIMAL TRACKS.

RACE, HUMAN see HUMAN BEING.

RACES see MARATHON RACE, TRACK AND FIELD.

RACHMANINOFF, SERGEI (1873–1943) Sergei Rachmaninoff was a Russian musician who won fame both as a concert pianist and as a composer. He was also a fine orchestra conductor.

Rachmaninoff was born on his family's estate near Novgorod, Russia. He studied music on a scholarship at the St. Petersburg Conservatory and later at the Moscow Conservatory. He met the great Russian composer, Peter Tchaikovsky, in Moscow. Tchaikovsky's works influenced Rachmaninoff's style.

Raccoons use their front paws like human hands. Indeed, raccoon tracks look very much like tiny human footprints.

▼ *This raccoon has made its home inside a hollow log. Raccoons also climb trees to make their dens in holes above ground. Others live and bring up their babies in rock crevices or on rocky ledges.*

▲ *Sergei Rachmaninoff,*
Russian composer.

Rachmaninoff's first symphony was so severely criticized that he stopped composing for a time. But he later wrote two other symphonies that were successful. Four concertos for piano and orchestra also brought him fame. Many pianists play his preludes and other piano solo pieces. Rachmaninoff's music has a powerful, brooding quality.

This talented musician was an exciting pianist to hear. He made many concert tours, playing especially his own works and those of Frédéric Chopin. Rachmaninoff left Russia in 1917 and never went back. Later, the United States became his permanent home. He became a citizen of the United States shortly before his death.

ALSO READ: COMPOSER; MUSIC; PIANO; TCHAIKOVSKY, PETER.

RACQUETBALL Racquetball is an indoor ball game played rather like handball, but, to hit the ball, the players use a racket (*racquet*) rather than their hands. The racket looks something like a small tennis racket.

Racquetball is a fast game that demands agility and speed. The players hit the ball, which is hollow and made of rubber, against the four walls and ceiling of the court. Two (singles) or four (doubles) may play. The game begins when the player on one side

▼ *Racquetball is a popular*
indoor sport. It demands
speed, strength, and
coordination.

serves by dropping the ball and hitting it on the first bounce against the front wall of the court. It must then be returned by the player or team on the other side before it bounces twice on the floor. The ball may hit the ceiling or any one of the walls, but it must hit the front wall before it touches the floor.

Points are scored by the serving side when the opposing side fails to return the ball. This continues as long as the serving side makes no error. When the serving side fails to serve or return properly, it loses the serve to the opposing side. The first player or team to score 21 points wins a game, and the first to win two games wins the match.

ALSO READ: SPORTS.

RADAR When waves hit something solid, they bounce back. If you shout into a well, or into the mouth of a cave, the sound waves of your voice bounce back as an echo. Radar, short for *ra*dio *d*etection *a*nd *r*anging, bounces radio waves off objects to find out where the objects are and where they are going.

A radar unit has an *antenna* (used for sending and receiving waves), a

▼ *Horizontal radar antennas are*
prominent fixtures at most air terminals.
The antennas send out and receive pulsing
radio waves from approaching aircraft.

transmitter, and a *receiver*. The transmitter sends out a wave pulse (a short bundle of waves). Radio waves travel at close to 186,000 miles (299,330 km) a second, so it doesn't take them long to get somewhere and back. When the waves hit a solid object, they bounce back to the radar unit.

The radar unit alternately switches off its transmitter and switches on its receiver. The transmitter and the receiver both use the same antenna, so they can't operate at the same time. The receiver picks up the returning waves and sends a signal to an indicator. The most common indicator is a *cathode ray tube*, an electronic tube having a screen much like a television screen. Objects appear as bright spots on the face of the tube. Lines on the tube show the distance and direction of the object.

Radar can also show how fast an object moves. When the waves bounce back from the object, their frequency (the number of waves per second) is changed, and the amount of change shows the speed. Some radar systems use continuous waves instead of pulses for this. A separate antenna must be used in addition to the transmitter.

Since radar uses radio waves, it can "see" anywhere radio waves can go. Radar can see through clouds and darkness, although it can pick up rain and other kinds of "solid" bad weather.

Radar was developed during World War II as an aid in tracking airplanes and finding targets. This is still one of the most important uses of radar. Radar can be used to aim a gun or missile at a target, or to detect missiles that are entering the area covered by the radar. Ships and planes carry radar to show them the position of other craft nearby. It is also used in weather forecasting and scientific research. The police use radar to measure the speed of vehicles in order to control speeding on the highways. Radar waves have been bounced off Venus

and Mars to help study and map those planets.

ALSO READ: AIR TRAFFIC CONTROL, PHYSICS, RADIO, RADIO ASTRONOMY.

RADIATION Sunlight, radio waves, and ripples on the surface of a body of water are all examples of radiation. Radiation is the way energy moves through substances or space.

Mechanical radiation is waves moving through *matter*—something that you can touch or feel, such as water or air. The matter the waves pass through is called the *medium*. The waves start when an object disturbs the medium. For instance, when a rock hits water it pushes particles (bits) of water out of the way. These particles move the particles next to them. In this way a wave moves across the water.

Waves of *electromagnetic* energy do not need a medium. Electromagnetic waves, such as light or radio waves, can travel through empty space. These waves are formed by the oscillations (vibrations) of electric and magnetic fields. Although they can travel through empty space, electromagnetic waves may change slightly when they pass through matter, or they may be absorbed (soaked up) by the matter. Electromagnetic waves travel through space at the speed of light, 186,000 miles (299,330 km) a second. The energy of a wave depends on its wavelength (distance between waves) and frequency (number

▲ *This Boeing AWACS (Airborne Warning and Control System) aircraft is one of many that patrol the skies day and night to detect enemy aircraft movements. These planes are a mass of radar equipment.*

▲ *Radar works by sending out radio signals that bounce off distant objects. The radar set detects the signals that return and produces a picture on a screen indicating the position of the objects.*

Radio waves can be as much as 10 miles (16 km) long. The waves given out by red light are only about .00003 of an inch (.000075 cm) long; the waves of violet light are only half the length of red waves. Other electromagnetic waves such as X rays and ultraviolet rays are very much shorter still.

Because these waves have such tiny lengths, scientists use a convenient unit when talking about them. This unit is the *ångström*. An ångström is one hundred-millionth of a centimeter. The wavelength of red light is therefore about 7,500 ångström.

▼ *The electromagnetic spectrum is made up of energy that moves in a wave motion at a fixed speed—that of light. The only difference between the various kinds of rays is their particular wavelength. Visible light, the only rays we can see, is at the center.*

of waves each second)—the longer the wavelength, the lower the frequency. Electromagnetic waves can have wavelengths as long as several miles, or so short that millions of waves could fit across a pinhead. The longest electromagnetic waves are radio waves, the shortest are gamma rays. In between are X rays, microwaves, infrared rays, visible light, and ultraviolet light.

Nuclear radiation is given off by the *nucleus* of an atom. It consists of electromagnetic radiation and streams of small particles. If the nucleus is hit by another particle, it may split and release nuclear radiation.

We could not live without radiation. If electromagnetic waves could not travel through empty space, the light and heat from the sun would never reach Earth. If the light (energy) from the sun could not reach the Earth, there would be no life here.

We could not hear or see without radiation. All the sounds that we hear travel to our ears in the form of mechanical radiation. All light travels as electromagnetic waves.

Radiation allows us to heat our homes, listen to the radio, and watch television. Radiation, such as X rays, is used in medicine.

ALSO READ: ELECTRICITY, NUCLEAR ENERGY, RADIOACTIVITY, SOUND, SPECTRUM, WAVE, X RAY.

RADIATION BELT Two distinct radiation belts, zones of electrically charged particles, circle the Earth like huge doughnuts. Dr. James Van Al-

▲ *This aerial photograph of Los Angeles was taken from space at night on film sensitive to infrared radiation. This type of photography is used in wartime to take pictures of blacked-out areas.*

len discovered the belts in 1958, from information collected by the first American satellite, Explorer I.

The inner belt begins about 400 miles (645 km) above the Earth's surface and extends outward to about 4,000 miles (6,450 km). This belt is thickest at the equator and thinnest at the poles. The outer belt begins about 8,000 miles (12,875 km) above the Earth and extends outward to about 12,000 miles (19,300 km).

The particles in the belts are held in place by the same force that pulls a compass needle toward north—the magnetic field of the Earth. Charged particles given off by the sun stream toward the Earth in a *solar wind*. When they hit the Earth's magnetic

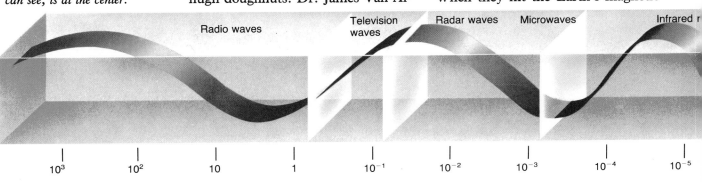

Radio waves Television waves Radar waves Microwaves Infrared r

10^3 10^2 10 1 10^{-1} 10^{-2} 10^{-3} 10^{-4} 10^{-5}

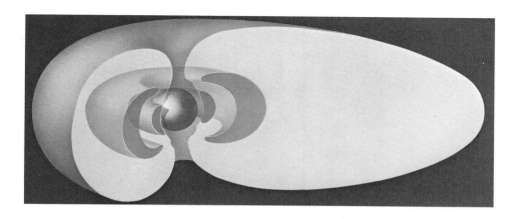

field, they are trapped and bounce back and forth inside the field, from north to south. Other particles, coming from outer space or from the Earth's atmosphere, may be trapped in the same way.

Radiation can make human beings and other animals sick and can damage electronic equipment. Spacecraft must pass through the belts quickly or have heavy shielding to block the radiation.

Other planets with strong magnetic fields, such as Jupiter, also have radiation belts.

ALSO READ: RADIATION, SPACE TRAVEL.

RADIO The sounds you listen to on a radio have had a very complicated journey. Suppose you are listening to an announcer reading the news over a radio. The announcer is sitting in a broadcasting studio miles from your home. The announcer speaks into a microphone. Inside the microphone is a thin sheet of metal. Each sound that strikes the sheet of metal makes it vibrate—or shake back and

forth very quickly. The metal vibrates a different way for each different sound that strikes it.

The microphone changes all these vibrations into very weak electrical signals, called *audio signals*. Each different kind of vibration produces a different audio signal.

The microphone is connected to a radio transmitter by an electric wire. Inside the radio transmitter is special equipment that makes the audio signals much stronger.

The transmitter also makes an electrical signal called a *carrier signal*. The radio transmitter then adds the audio signals to the carrier signal. Adding the audio signal to the carrier is called *modulating* the carrier. The modulation can be either *amplitude* modulation (AM radio) or *frequency* modulation (FM radio). In amplitude modulation, adding the audio signal changes the height of the carrier signal. In frequency modulation, the audio signal changes the instant of time between carrier signals. Finally, the radio transmitter sends the modulated carrier signal to a large radio antenna. As the modulated carrier

The first radio broadcast to contain speech and music was made on December 24, 1906, in the United States. The broadcast was given by the Canadian inventor Reginald Fessenden, who talked, sang, and played the violin. The first actual radio station began operating in New York in 1907.

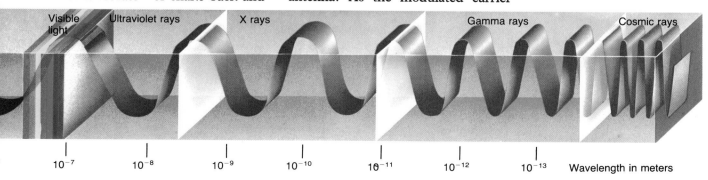

Visible light   Ultraviolet rays   X rays   Gamma rays   Cosmic rays

10^{-7} 10^{-8} 10^{-9} 10^{-10} 10^{-11} 10^{-12} 10^{-13} Wavelength in meters

RADIO

▶ *How radio waves travel.*
Short waves shoot upward and
are reflected down by the
ionosphere. VHF waves can
be sent over the horizon by
high transmitting and receiving
antennas. Super-high
frequency radio waves shoot
out into space but can be
reflected back by satellites.

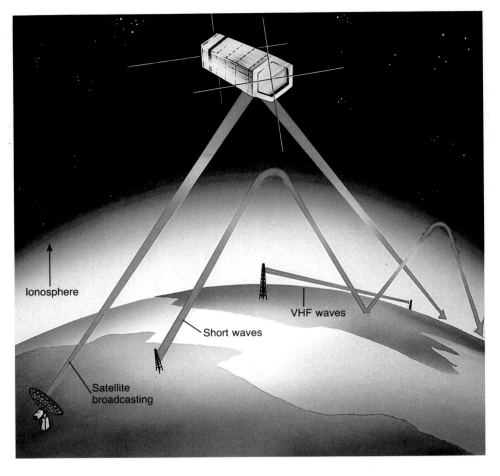

Ionosphere

Short waves

VHF waves

Satellite
broadcasting

**Radio waves travel at
the speed of light. This
is so fast that a signal
can travel around the
Earth 7½ times in
one second.**

**The first radio stations
were owned and run by
manufacturers of radio
sets. The manufacturers
had to broadcast the
programs, otherwise
people would have had
no reason to buy
the radios.**

travels through the antenna, it gives off radio waves. The radio waves move out in all directions at the speed of light, 186,000 miles (299, 330 km) a second.

A carrier signal and the carrier wave it produces vibrate thousands of times every second. You can compare a carrier signal with a whistle. The whistling sound is also made up of vibrations. These vibrations travel through the air. Now, if you made a steady whistling noise that did not change at all, this noise would be like the carrier signal that a radio transmitter makes. Start to whistle a tune now. In a way, you have added the tune to the whistling sound. Something like this happens inside the radio transmitter when the announcer's voice is added to the carrier signal. The carrier signal with the announcer's voice added to it is sent into the air as radio waves to be picked up by the receiving antenna.

Inside Your Radio When radio waves strike the antenna of your radio, the antenna turns the waves back into very weak electrical signals again. These electrical signals travel from the antenna into the radio.

The radio makes these weak electrical signals much stronger. The radio also separates the carrier signal from the audio signals that carry the sounds made by the announcer. Finally, the radio sends these audio signals to a loudspeaker. The signals make the loudspeaker vibrate. The loudspeaker vibrates in exactly the same way as the thin piece of metal in the microphone. These vibrations leave the loudspeaker and travel through the air. When the vibrations strike your ears, you hear the vibrations as sounds.

As you know, you can pick out many different radio stations on the radio. You pick a station by turning a knob on the front of the radio. This is called "tuning" a radio to a station. What you are doing is choosing one carrier from among all the different carrier signals being transmitted.

When radio was first invented, the people who wanted to build radio transmitters used whatever carrier signals they wanted to. If two people used the same carrier signal, their radio signals got mixed up. If you tried to tune your radio to one of these stations, you would hear the other station also. It is the same as if two people tried to whistle two different songs at the same time. Other people would find it hard to distinguish between the songs.

To prevent this kind of confusion, the U.S. government established the Federal Communications Commission, or FCC. The FCC told every radio station what carrier signal it could use. Now the radio stations cannot interfere with each other.

The numbers on the dial of a radio identify the carrier signals assigned to each radio station. When you "tune" a radio, what you are actually doing is choosing a particular carrier signal to listen to.

▼ *In AM radio, the amplitude (size) of the carrier wave varies in relation to the sound signal. In FM, the amplitude remains constant, but the frequency varies with the sound signal. FM broadcasting gives better sound quality.*

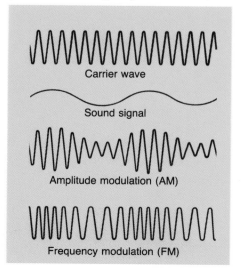

Carrier wave

Sound signal

Amplitude modulation (AM)

Frequency modulation (FM)

Each station's carrier signal has a different wavelength (distance between waves) and frequency (number of waves each second). AM stations transmit long wavelengths at low frequencies. FM stations transmit shorter wavelengths at higher frequencies. "Short-wave" stations transmit wavelengths shorter than AM but longer than FM. Short waves can be broadcast for thousands of miles, so they are used for long-range communications and international broadcasting. Radio amateurs send short-wave messages all over the world.

ALSO READ: ELECTRICITY, RADIATION, RADIO BROADCASTING, SOUND, SPECTRUM, TELEVISION, WAVE.

RADIO, AMATEUR Have you ever listened to faraway stations on a shortwave radio? Radio amateurs, or "hams," can both listen and talk to stations all over the world.

A ham radio station has a *transmitter*, for sending radio signals; a *receiver*, for receiving signals; and an *antenna*. Some hams build their own stations from kits, while others buy their equipment ready-made. A complete station can be small enough to fit on a desk, or large enough to fill a room.

Amateur radio is the only hobby that is regulated by national and international law. In order to become a ham, you must first get a license from the government. Most hams begin with a *novice* license. To get this license you have to pass a simple test. Novices can use only code on their stations. Children as young as six have received licenses. The next step is either a *technician class* license or a *general class* license. These allow you to talk with other hams. Experienced amateurs can obtain more advanced licenses.

In 1958, the U.S. government set aside certain radio frequencies as the

▲ *From the bulky radiograms of the 1930's, radios have become sophisticated and miniaturized pieces of equipment using the latest technology. They are often combined with portable cassette players such as this.*

▲ *Citizen's band radio (CB) is popular with car and truck drivers. The sets operate on several channels within the band. The signals are weak so that they do not carry very far.*

Citizens Band. This band has become very popular with emergency personnel, with truck drivers, and with many others who use it for business, for reporting emergencies, and just for conversation. No technical knowledge is required to use a "CB" radio, and the operator needs no license though his or her radio does. CB operators have a colorful language of their own, and listening to them can be very amusing. *Transceivers* (transmitters and receivers) are sold in many stores. License applications come with them for the new owner's convenience.

ALSO READ: MORSE CODE, RADIO, RADIO BROADCASTING.

RADIOACTIVITY If you look through a magnifying glass at a watch dial that glows in the dark, you will see that the glowing is made up of tiny flickers of light. The dial has been painted with an element (basic substance) called *radium*, and the flickers of light are caused by *radiation*—bundles of energy given off by the radium because it is *radioactive.*

All elements are made up of atoms. Millions of atoms could fit on the dot of this "i." Every atom has a nucleus—a small, hard, inner core—and electrons—negative electrical charges that circle the nucleus the way the moon circles the Earth.

A nucleus is not all one piece. It is made up of protons—heavy particles with positive electrical charges—and neutrons—heavy particles with no electrical charge. The number of protons in an atom determines what element it is. An element is radioactive because its nucleus is unstable—it tends to decay, or break apart.

When a radium atom decays it gives off an *alpha particle*—a bundle of two protons and two neutrons. Because it has lost two protons, the atom is no longer an atom of radium. It is now an atom of another element,

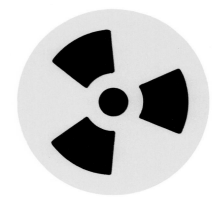

▲ *This radiation sign is used to warn people of radioactivity.*

called *radon.* Radon is radioactive, too. The radon atom eventually gives off an alpha particle and becomes a polonium atom.

Radium, radon, and polonium are just three steps in a long chain of radioactive decay, starting with uranium and ending up with lead, which is not radioactive. Not all of the radioactive elements give off alpha particles. Some of them give off *beta particles*—electrons made in the nucleus. The emission of alpha and beta particles is often accompanied by the emission of *gamma rays.* Gamma rays are electromagnetic waves. They act like bundles of energy that fly through space at the speed of light.

The energy given off by a decaying nucleus is tremendous, considering the small size of the atom. The radioactive decay of one ounce (28 g) of uranium gives off as much energy as the burning of 50,000 pounds (22,680 kg) of coal. A radioactive element can be made to decay all at once, as in a nuclear bomb, but in nature only a few atoms decay at a time. The rate of decay of an element is called the element's *half-life*—this is the amount of time it takes for half of the atoms to decay. The half-life of most natural uranium is 4½ billion years. What was an ounce (28 g) of uranium 4½ billion years ago is now only half an ounce (14 g). The other half ounce has decayed into other elements and energy. Not all radioactive elements

The nucleus of a nonradioactive element

Protons

Nucleus of radioactive element

Escaping particle

Neutrons

▲ *The nucleus of a radioactive element contains many protons and neutrons packed together. These particles do not like being packed together in large numbers, so some may leave the nucleus, making the element radioactive.*

have half-lives as long as uranium. Polonium has a half-life of less than a millionth of a second.

The half-lives of radioactive substances can be useful in dating (finding out the age of) things. All organisms (living things) contain carbon, and all carbon contains some carbon 14. Carbon 14 is a radioactive *isotope* of carbon—it has the same number of protons but a different number of neutrons. Carbon 14 is made in our atmosphere by the action of sunlight on carbon. Once an organism dies, it takes in no more carbon 14 from the air. When it is buried underground, no more of its carbon changes into carbon 14. The carbon 14 it already has decays into plain carbon. By measuring the proportion of carbon 14 in the fossils (buried remains) of organisms, scientists can tell how long they have been dead.

Radioactivity was discovered in 1896 by the French scientist, Antoine Henri Becquerel. Becquerel noticed that a piece of uranium could blacken a photographic plate, even when black paper was put between them. The blackening was caused by the radiation from the uranium. Two

▼ *Curium 242, an isotope of the element curium, is radioactive. As it decays, it gives off radiation. The energy of the decay produces heat and light.*

other French scientists, Marie and Pierre Curie, gave this radiation the name "radioactivity," and discovered that radioactivity was a property of the uranium itself, and not the result of chemical action.

Radioactivity is a very useful but dangerous phenomenon (fact). Small doses of radioactivity can be used to cure diseases, but larger doses are poisonous. Controlled radioactivity (nuclear energy) can provide the power to run ships, factories, and cities. Uncontrolled radioactivity has the power to destroy. The most serious accident so far in the field of nuclear energy occurred in April 1986 at the Chernobyl Power Plant in the Soviet Union. The core of the nuclear reactor overheated when the cooling system failed, and an explosion released a cloud of radiation that spread far from the plant. Radioactive levels rose in many European countries. By May, 23 people had died as a result of the disaster. Long term effects of the high radioactivity were still unknown.

ALSO READ: ATOM, CURIE FAMILY, ELEMENT, FALLOUT, GEIGER COUNTER, NUCLEAR ENERGY, RADIATION.

▲ *Gamma rays from a radioisotope (left) are used to examine an airplane engine. The rays pass through the engine intake and expose films around the outside (shown being placed in position). The pictures show up any faults in the engine.*

The alpha particles given off by radioactive substances are not a great danger to people because they are stopped by the outer layer of the skin. Beta particles are more penetrating and can get inside the skin. Gamma rays are like very strong X rays and can easily penetrate matter. They pass right through the human body and can cause harm to the atoms inside.

▲ *The world's largest fully steerable radio telescope, at Effelsberg, in West Germany, has a reflecting dish 328 feet (100 m) across. It receives radio emission from objects ranging from the whispering cool clouds of hydrogen in our own galaxy to the strident quasars that seem to signal from the edge of the universe.*

A powerful radio telescope on top of Mauna Kea in Hawaii is picking up signals from galaxies 10 trillion miles away. The telescope is designed to receive signals as small as one-fourth of a Jansky. A Jansky is a unit so small that an instrument capable of detecting one Jansky could pick up the energy given out by a warm pebble on the moon!

RADIO ASTRONOMY Only a small part of the universe can be seen with even the most powerful optical (visual) telescope. A much larger part of the universe can be "heard" by using a radio telescope. A radio telescope is not at all like an optical telescope. It is like a huge radio antenna. However, the radio waves that are heard with a radio telescope are not very different from the light waves that are seen with an optical telescope. They are both forms of electromagnetic radiation—energy that travels through space in waves. Some bodies in space give off light waves, some give off radio waves, and some give off both. Radiation is our contact with the universe. We could not know of the existence of a body that did not give off radiation.

Different substances give off different kinds of radiation. Hydrogen, probably the most common element in the universe, gives off radio waves with a wavelength of 21 centimeters (8¼ inches). When a radio telescope picks up a radio wave with a wavelength of 21 centimeters, the astrono-

mers suspect that hydrogen is present. Radio astronomy has helped astronomers to construct a map of the hydrogen in our galaxy. Radio waves can also tell astronomers how hot the surface of an object is. Different temperatures have different wavelengths.

If a body gives off more radio waves than light, an astronomer can learn more about its make-up by listening to it than by looking at it. Quasars (quasi-stellar radio sources) give off little light but very strong radio waves. Their waves show a shift (change) in wavelength that suggests that some are moving away at 150,000 miles (241,400 km) a second. We are still not sure what quasars are, but they may be galaxies at the far edge of the known universe.

The antenna of a radio telescope looks like a huge dish or the blade of a snow shovel. The antenna picks up the radio waves and a *radiometer* measures their intensity (strength). Radio waves from space can have wavelengths of less than an inch (2.5 cm) or more than 50 feet (15 m). To catch the larger waves, several antennas are put side by side in a long row. A radio telescope with several antennas is called an *interferometer*. Some are more than a mile (1.6 km) long and are often cross-shaped. Interferometers help astronomers locate wave sources. Information from interferometers thousands of miles apart may be compared.

Radio waves from space were first detected by the American astronomer, Karl Jansky, in 1932. Shortly afterwards, one of Jansky's students, Grote Reber, built the first radio telescope. It had a 10-foot-wide (3-m-wide) dish-shaped antenna. Today, the largest dish-shaped radio telescope, dug out of limestone in Arecibo, Puerto Rico, is 1,000 feet (305 m) across. The largest radio telescope of any kind was completed in 1981 at Socorro, New Mexico. It is Y-shaped with each arm 13 miles (21 km) long with 27 mobile antennas on rails.

ALSO READ: ASTRONOMY, OBSERVATORY, RADIO, STAR.

RADIO BROADCASTING

In 1922, there were only 600 radio broadcasting stations in operation in the United States. By 1985, the number had increased to over 9,500.

Radio broadcasting is a way of communicating to a large audience by sending radio programs over the air. Communication devices that reach very large audiences are called *mass media*. Radio broadcasting is one of the *mass media*. By combining voices, music, and sound effects, radio broadcasters have developed ways of broadcasting news, sports events, drama, music, and advertisements. Because you cannot see a picture on radio, broadcasters try to arouse the listeners' imagination and get them to picture things.

Among the pioneers in radio development were Heinrich Hertz, a German physicist, and Lee De Forest, an American inventor. Hertz's experiments with electromagnetic waves led to the development of wireless radio. De Forest designed a number of transmitters and, in 1916, reported the results of the Presidential election in the first radio news broadcast.

Radio Entertainment From the 1920's to 1950's, radio stations offered a wide range of programs—variety shows, radio drama, mysteries, westerns, comedy shows, plus many others. Television has taken over most of these types of programs, and radio is now pretty much limited to news, music, and special broadcasts (such as sports events, operas, discussion programs, and so on). Radio programs are still very popular, however. About 85 percent of all Americans listen to radio at least once a day. People listen to radio as they drive their cars. Many people take portable transistor radios on picnics or to the beach. Sometimes you can hear radio broadcasts piped over speakers in stores and office buildings. And of course many people listen to radio in their homes, especially for music and news.

On Sunday mornings, local radio stations broadcast church services and religious discussion programs, as well as news and music. Some stations specialize in broadcasting only news, classical or popular music, educational shows, or foreign language programs.

Radio Frequency All radio stations that broadcast in the United States must be licensed by the Federal Communications Commission. By granting a license, the FCC permits the station to use a particular airwave frequency. According to law, all U.S. airwaves are owned by the people. The government simply gives permission for broadcasters to use them. The FCC license must be renewed every three years. If a station broadcasts programs that are in some way harmful to people, the broadcaster's license is taken away. The National Association of Radio and Television Broadcasters (an organization of licensed station owners) has set up rules about the kinds of programs appropriate for broadcasting.

You can tune to two types of radio stations—AM (amplitude modulation) or FM (frequency modulation). The initials AM and FM indicate the

▲ *Radio astronomy has enabled us to "listen" to very distant but very powerful bodies such as quasars, billions of light-years away.*

▼ *Scene in a radio studio in the 1940's. The soundproof control booth is at the rear.*

▲ *Reading the news. The announcer receives instructions from the control room through the headphones.*

▼ *An array of buttons, slides and other modern broadcasting equipment surround this radio announcer at station WNBC, New York.*

type of airwave over which a station broadcasts. AM radio waves move in waves that are very high. There is a greater distance between the high and low points of an AM wave than of an FM wave. FM radio waves move in waves that are very wide. There is a greater distance between each of the outer points of an FM wave.

Radio Industry In the United States, broadcasting is a business in which station owners try to make a profit. Station owners sell *air time* (broadcast time) to businesses that use the time to advertise their products. Stations also get advertisers to *sponsor* shows (pay the cost of entire programs) in exchange for radio advertising time.

In some nations, such as the Soviet Union, Poland, and Denmark, all radio and television stations are owned and run by the government. Government-owned stations do not need advertising. Nations such as Great Britain have stations that are not run by the government directly. The British government has licensed a *public service company* called the British Broadcasting Corporation. The cost of programs is paid for by setting up a tax on all radio and television sets. The government gives these tax revenues to the BBC, and the corporation provides radio and television programs with the money.

A radio *network* is a combination of widely spaced stations that agree to carry the same programs in exchange for fees paid by advertisers whose commercials are broadcast over the network. Belonging to a network saves local stations from having to create shows and get advertisers for every program they broadcast. Radio stations do not need to belong to networks because they can often support themselves with money from local advertisers. There are four national radio networks in the United States.

If you would like to work in radio broadcasting someday, there are many different types of jobs you could do. Radio *announcers* report the news, work as disc jockeys, give play-by-play descriptions of sports events, and often broadcast commercials. *Producers* decide which radio programs to broadcast. They locate sponsors and hire the announcers, interviewers, and other broadcast talent. Radio *directors* actually direct the progress of a radio broadcast. Radio *engineers* operate the equipment that sends broadcasts out over the airwaves. *Writers* create scripts for radio shows, such as news broadcasts. Writers are also employed by advertisers to write commercial messages for broadcast on the air. Radio stations also have *librarians*. A librarian keeps track of a radio station's large collection of phonograph records and tape-recorded material.

You might like to visit a radio station to see an actual broadcast in operation. The announcer sits in a soundproof room and speaks through a microphone. The engineer monitors (listens to) the broadcast as it goes out over the air to correct any distortion in sound or to add special electronic effects to the sound when needed. The director gives the announcer cues about when to begin speaking, when a commercial or station break must be announced, and many other things.

Directors and announcers must

make sure there is no *dead air time* (long pauses without any sound coming over the air). If the station has dead spots in its broadcasts, people tuning in will not realize that the station is on the air. It is for this reason that announcers keep talking, no matter what. Good announcers must be able to talk about anything on the spur of the moment to keep the airwaves alive.

ALSO READ: COMMUNICATION; RADIO; RADIO, AMATEUR; TELEVISION; TELEVISION BROADCASTING.

RAILROAD Before the invention of the automobile and the airplane, railroads were the fastest and most widely used method of carrying mail, food, fuel, other freight, and passengers from place to place. Today, railroads are still a major means of freight shipment, but they are not the "kings" of transportation they once were. A railroad is really a transportation network, rather than simply a vehicle for transportation. A great deal of equipment, thousands of workers, and miles of tracks and railroad cars go into making a railroad.

Certain railroad employees work aboard a train. The *engineer* runs the locomotive. The *fireman* assists the engineer. The *conductor* is in charge of all the train except the locomotive.

Trainmen or *brakemen* assist the conductor. Porters wait on passengers. But many other people—off the train—are needed to keep a railroad running. A repair crew keeps cars and locomotives in running condition. *Dispatchers* determine the routes trains will follow and signal the engineers on trains. Station employees sell tickets and load freight and baggage.

Classification Yards Trains are made up in *classification yards*, where the necessary cars are coupled together and attached to locomotives. In automatically controlled classification yards, cars are switched with electric "eyes," which pick up codes on the cars and route them to the proper track. The *rolling stock* (cars and locomotives) is cleaned, repaired, and refueled in other yards.

Signals and Controls Railroads have complicated systems of automatic and manual signals that control the routing, braking, and, in some cases, even the speed of trains on their tracks. Dispatchers are railroad employees who control all train routes. They control the electric light signals that appear over the tracks and, in some cases, in the locomotive cabs. These lights either form lines set in different ways or show different colors that tell the locomotive driver "Stop," "Caution," or "Go."

The first passenger train in America made its initial trip from Charleston, South Carolina to Hamburg, South Carolina in 1830. The newspaper account of the trip read: "The passengers flew on wings of the wind. . .at the fantastic speed of 15 miles an hour."

In November 1967, six diesel locomotives of the Norfolk and Western Railway pulled the longest freight train ever. It consisted of 500 coal cars and stretched for about 4 miles (6 km).

▼ *A controller (below left), in radio contact with classification yard staff, operates switches to bring together cars with the same destination. Big yards, such as the one below, may be controlled by computer.*

▲ *An old hand-operated switch alongside a railroad track. Modern switches are automatically operated from a control tower.*

▲ *Signals control the movement of trains. They keep trains away from each other, and they also help to keep them running efficiently and on time.*

▶ *A modern signal box switchboard controls a large section of track. A dispatcher sets switches and changes signals as lights show him where each train is.*

The Centralized Traffic Control System is a modern way of handling railroad communication. Under this system, the position of the trains is shown continuously on an electric diagram in front of the dispatcher, who sends signals to engineers with special equipment in the control tower. The CTC system also uses radio for communication between the dispatcher and engineer. Microwave communication is one of the newest developments in the railroad industry. Microwave messages are sent from the control tower to saucer-shaped receivers on pedestals above the train track. These receivers then send the messages (received in the form of flashing lights in the locomotive cab) to passing trains.

Some short-distance, or commuter, railroads operate under a system of automatic train control. In this system, an electric master control is located in the front of the locomotive just above the rails. The master control picks up electric current in the rails and interprets the kind of electric signal it has received. Then the master control tells the engineer what should be done by braking, flashing lights, or sounding bells. The master control also determines how fast the train can be operated.

Types of Cars and Locomotives

FREIGHT CARS. The railroad industry makes most of its money from shipping freight. There are freight cars to carry almost anything. *Boxcars* are covered cars used to ship material that simply needs protection from weather and loss. *Flatcars* consist of a floor attached to the wheels, without sides or top. Flatcars are used for carrying heavy, wide loads—such as logs—that will not be harmed by exposure to the weather. *Tank cars* are cylindrical-shaped, covered cars built for carrying liquids, such as oil. *Refrigerator cars* carry food products that would spoil in ordinary boxcars. *Hoppers*, either open-top or closed, are funnel-shaped cars that carry materials such as coal, grain, or gravel. *Auto-rack cars* contain either two or three racks for transporting automobiles. *"Piggy-back"* cars carry the trailer (but not the cab) of a large truck. Goods can be shipped rapidly over long distances by piggy-back. At the railroad station nearest the destination, the trailer is attached to a truck cab. The rest of the trip is then made by truck. This method of shipment is known as Tructrain service. A *unit train* is made up of cars carrying the same product. Unit trains often save a railroad time and money. The *caboose*, the last car in a freight train, contains sleeping quarters and a kitchen for the train crew.

PASSENGER SERVICE. The two main types of passenger trains in operation today are *commuter trains* and *intercity trains*. Commuter trains (between a city and its suburbs) carry millions of people to and from work in such cities as New York City, Chicago, Tokyo, Paris and London. This is often referred to as *rapid transit*. Intercity trains (for example, from New York to Washington, D.C.) travel at a high speed and make longer runs than commuter trains do. Fast intercity trains serve cities in Japan, France, the Soviet Union, Canada, the United States, and other coun-

▲ *A German diesel-electric locomotive. The smokestack on top is for exhaust fumes from the engine.*

tries. These trains may have *sleeping*, or *Pullman*, *cars* for long trips. Some trains have *dining cars*. *Club cars* or *observation cars* are lounges where passengers can go to relax and look at the scenery. Some observation cars have windows around one end of the car and a higher viewing deck to give passengers the best view possible.

LOCOMOTIVES. The locomotive consists of the engine and a cab for the engineer. The locomotive is mounted on wheels like other cars and provides the power that moves an entire train. The earliest locomotives, *steam locomotives*, were powered by steam engines. *Diesel locomotives*, first used in the 1920's and still in use, are more efficient than steam locomotives in converting fuel to mechanical energy, and diesels do not require so many fuel stops. *Electric locomotives* are cleaner and more efficient than diesels are. But electric locomotives need to get electric current from wires suspended above the track or an electrified third rail. *Diesel-electric locomotives* run on electricity produced by their own oil-burning diesel engines. These locomotives are the most widely used in the United States today. Other types of locomotives include *gas-turbine electric locomotives* and *diesel-hydraulic locomotives*.

Early Railroads The earliest railroads were wagon ways built in mines in the 1500's and 1600's to haul out coal, ore, or stone. These railroads consisted of horse-drawn wagons traveling over wooden rails. *Crossties* (wooden beams or ties) were introduced to hold the rails in place, and the wooden tracks were soon replaced with iron ones. But horses, donkeys, or mules supplied the power until the beginning of the 1800's, when steam locomotives first came into use. The first practical locomotive was built in 1804 by the English engineer, Richard Trevithick. Another Englishman, George Stephenson, improved the locomotive by returning the steam that escaped back into the engine. This increased the steam pressure in the engine, making it more powerful. Future steam locomotives were built according to Stephenson's example.

Commercial railroading began with the opening of the Stockton-Darlington Line in England in 1825. In 1830, the Charleston and Hamburg Railroad became the first American line to use steam locomotives. The Baltimore and Ohio (begun in 1830) began using steam locomotives the following year. France and Germany built railroads soon after, as did Russia, India, Australia, Africa, and other parts of the world. By 1900, one could cross America or Russia by train, or go from Paris to Istanbul.

When railroads first came into general use, railroad operators discovered some problems they had not anticipated. The width (gauge) between tracks varied from one railroad to another. This meant that the trains of one railroad could not run on the tracks of another railroad. The problem was solved by standardizing the gauge for all tracks. In the United States and many other countries, the standard gauge is 4 feet 8½ inches (1.4 m). In America, where tracks ran through wild, open country, an unlit track could be dangerous at night. At first, trains pushed ahead of them a

▲ *Loading freight into standard-size containers to be lifted by crane from trucks onto piggy-back cars makes it easier for the system to be controlled from a computer.*

Most railroad gauges in the world measure 4 feet 8½ inches (1.4 m). This was the gauge of the Durham colliery in England on which the very first train ran. It also seems to have been the gauge between the wheels of ancient Roman carts, as their ruts can still be measured in places like Pompeii.

▶ *The* Lafayette, *built in 1837, is an early locomotive still preserved in working order by the Baltimore and Ohio Railroad.*

▼ *How a steam locomotive works.*

2 The **boiler** in front of the firebox is filled with water to be turned into steam. **Boiler flue tubes** carry hot gases from the firebox through the boiler to heat the water. Steam collects in the space above the water.

3 **Safety valve** to let off excess steam

4 The **smokebox** and its chimney draw hot gases through the boiler tubes from the firebox, providing a draft for the fire

1 The **firebox** usually burns coal, sometimes wood or oil

11 A **sand box** scatters sand on the rails in front of or behind the driving wheels to give them extra grip when starting forward or in reverse

10 **Connecting rods** link front, middle, and rear wheels together, making six driving wheels in all

9 The **driving rod** of each piston turns a driving wheel. On this locomotive, two outside cylinders drive the middle pair of driving wheels; two inside cylinders drive the front pair

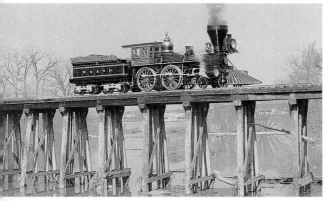

▲ *The* General, *the most famous locomotive of the Civil War.*

▲ *One of the Union Pacific's "Big Boys," built in the early 1940's and considered to be the largest of all steam locomotives.*

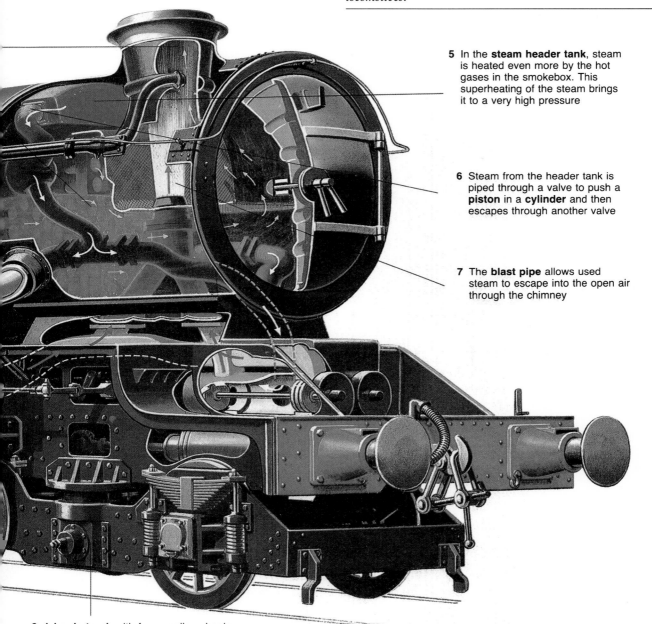

5 In the **steam header tank**, steam is heated even more by the hot gases in the smokebox. This superheating of the steam brings it to a very high pressure

6 Steam from the header tank is piped through a valve to push a **piston** in a **cylinder** and then escapes through another valve

7 The **blast pipe** allows used steam to escape into the open air through the chimney

8 A **bogie truck** with four smaller wheels at the front of the locomotive allows it to take bends smoothly

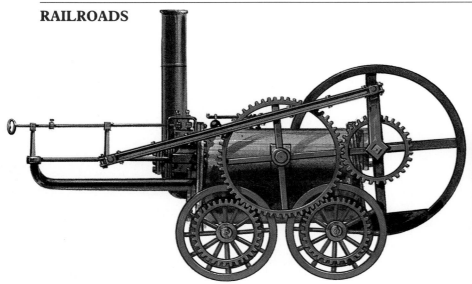

▲ *The building of the railroads was a tough, back-breaking job in which men labored long and hard to lay tracks to link areas of the United States.*

▲ *Richard Trevithick's original locomotive, which pioneered the railroad age in 1804.*

▼ *Railroads in the United States were important to the growth of the country after the Civil War. This is the station at Harrisburg, Pennsylvania, in the late 1860's.*

flatcar of burning wood to provide light. Later, until electric lights came into use, a kerosene lamp with a reflector was attached to the front of the locomotive. Railroad operators had trouble with animals straying onto the track until the cowcatcher was invented. This was a frame attached to the lower front of the locomotive to clear the track ahead.

Railroads played a very important part in the rapid western expansion and industrial growth of the United States in the second half of the 1800's. People could go at least part of the way to newly settled territories by rail. When workers on the Central Pacific and Union Pacific railroads met at Promontory Point, Utah, on May 10, 1869, they joined the rails of the two lines, creating a coast-to-coast railroad. Business and agriculture in new territories and states depended for survival upon rail shipment of

their goods. Railroads also influenced the pattern of growth and settlement in the West. People tended to settle near railroads, so towns grew up there.

The Federal Government (and later, local governments) helped railroads grow by giving them grants of land on which to build tracks. But during the second half of the 1800's, railroad owners began dishonest and unfair practices in building, charging for freight, and competing with other railroads. The public had few defenses because they needed railroads for transportation and freight shipment. But people began demanding laws to restrict the industry. In 1887, the Interstate Commerce Commission (ICC) was formed to regulate and control such railroad practices.

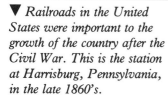

Railroads of the Future Some kind of high-speed ground transportation is needed to relieve the heavy automobile traffic in cities and on highways. Railroads are working on this problem. A few countries, such as Japan and France, have already developed efficient, comfortable, high-speed railroads. Engineers have been working for years on the *monorail*, a series of passenger-carrying vehicles (similar to railroad cars) suspended from a rail. (A monorail runs some feet above the ground.) Monorails are still experimental, although one has been in operation in West Germany since 1901. Monorails have been used at several world's fairs. If they prove practical, commercial monorails may be built in many places in the United States.

In the middle of this century, railroads began to lose a great deal of their business to newer and faster methods of transportation—automobiles, trucks, and airplanes. But with improved methods (such as the piggyback car) and more efficient service, railroads have won back some freight business, their major source of income.

Most U.S. passenger service now consists of commuter lines, serving the nation's major urban centers. At the same time, intercity passenger service is being reestablished. In 1971, a federal organization called Amtrak took over the operation of most U.S. intercity passenger trains. Federal government spending on railroads is still low compared to spend-

ing on highway construction and air and water transportation.

ALSO READ: SUBWAY, TRANSPORTATION.

RAIN AND SNOW You know that rain and snow fall from clouds. Have you ever wondered how raindrops and snowflakes happen to be in clouds?

Clouds are made up of tiny droplets of water. The average droplet is only 34 millionths of an inch (0.0009 mm) in diameter. It is so light that it hangs in the air, moving downward very slowly. The air in a cloud is always moving around. This causes some of the droplets to bump into others. The bumping droplets join together, forming larger droplets. The weight of a larger droplet enables it to overcome the movements of air. The

▲ *In most European countries, the busiest lines are electrified. Electric trains are cheap to operate, but the trackside equipment they need is expensive.*

▼ *The French* Aérotrain *(below left) glides along on a layer of air a few millimeters thick. The French* TGV (train à grande vitesse) *below is one of the world's fastest high-speed passenger trains.*

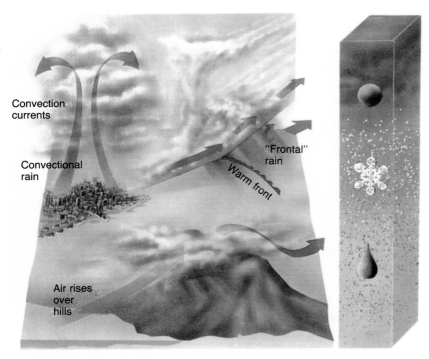

Convection currents

Convectional rain

Air rises over hills

"Frontal" rain

Warm front

▲ *Rain forms as warm, water-laden air rises or meets cooler air. The water in the air condenses into tiny droplets that form clouds.*

▼ *Rainbows often appear at waterfalls as the sun's light shines on the heavy spray. The droplets act like a prism, splitting the sun's light into a full spectrum of color.*

droplet falls faster and faster. It bumps into more and more droplets and grows larger and larger. Most rain clouds are very high from top to bottom. Before a falling droplet reaches the bottom of a cloud, it may be made up of a million tiny droplets and be one-twentieth of an inch (1.3 mm) in diameter. It has become a raindrop. It may grow to one-quarter of an inch. The joining of water droplets until they are heavy enough to fall is the way raindrops usually form in the tropics.

In the temperate regions of the Earth, the tops of rain clouds are cold enough for tiny ice crystals to form. The falling crystals pick up water droplets and other ice crystals. Snowflakes are formed. By the time the snowflakes reach the lower and warmer parts of the cloud, they melt and form raindrops.

If the temperature of a whole cloud is below freezing, and the temperature of the air on the ground is also below freezing, snow falls on the ground. Each snow crystal has a different, lacy design and six sides or points.

The amount of rain, snow, sleet, hail, or other moisture that falls is called *precipitation*, a term often used by those who report the weather.

ALSO READ: CLOUD, FOG, FROST, HAIL, HUMIDITY, WEATHER.

RAINBOW After a storm, tiny drops of water often remain in the air. When sunlight enters a water drop, it is *refracted*—bent and broken into colors. Then it is reflected off the inside of the drop, and when it leaves the drop, it is refracted again. The light is bent because light travels at a different speed in water than it does in air. The light is broken into colors because different colors of light travel at different speeds in water.

After refraction, the different colors of light leave the drops at different angles and appear at different angles in the sky. If you are looking in the direction of the drops, you will see bands of color arched across the sky. You will see a rainbow.

■ LEARN BY DOING

You can make a rainbow yourself on a sunny day. All you need is a water hose with a spray nozzle. Stand with your back to the sun and spray the water away from you. You should be able to see a rainbow in the spray. What happens when you hold the hose at different angles? When you vary the spray? ■

ALSO READ: COLOR, LIGHT, SPECTRUM.

RAIN FOREST see JUNGLE.

RALEIGH, SIR WALTER (1552–1618) Sir Walter Raleigh was an English adventurer, army commander, explorer, colonizer, and writer. He established one of the first colonies in North America, on Roanoke Island, North Carolina.

Raleigh began his career as a soldier. He fought with the Protestant

Huguenots against the Catholics in France and for the British in Ireland. From 1578 to 1580, Raleigh and his half brother, Sir Humphrey Gilbert, went to sea to raid Spanish shipping in America.

Raleigh was a poet and also wrote about travel and history. He soon became a favorite of Queen Elizabeth I. She made him a knight and commissioned him to seek new lands for England in the Americas. In 1585, Raleigh sent a group of about 100 men to Roanoke Island. The men did not develop farms or befriend the Indians. When Sir Francis Drake passed by the next year, they begged to be taken back to England.

Raleigh sent more colonists in 1587. When supply ships came in 1591, there was no trace of these settlers. To this day the mystery of the "Lost Colony" has never been solved.

Raleigh's efforts to establish colonies in America brought England much information about the geography, Indians, and plants of the New World. He introduced tobacco and potatoes to Europe.

In 1595, Raleigh led an exploring trip to Guiana in South America. His ships went up the Orinoco River in what is now Venezuela. During the war with Spain in the 1590's, Raleigh's leadership as an admiral on the flagship, *Warspite*, helped the English capture the main Spanish seaport of Cadiz.

Raleigh was out of favor at court when King James came to the throne. The king wanted peace with Spain. In 1603, the king had Raleigh imprisoned for treason. In prison, he wrote a book called *History of the World*. After 13 years, he was released and allowed to search for gold in Guiana on the condition that he would not attack the Spanish. But his men fought with the Spanish and Raleigh's son, Wat, was killed. When Raleigh returned to England, the king ordered him beheaded for disobeying

orders and attacking the Spanish. Fearless to the end, Raleigh joked with the executioner and gave the signal for the ax to fall.

ALSO READ: ELIZABETH I, EXPLORATION.

RANCHING When settlers first moved westward into the Great Plains they found vast areas of government-owned land known as the open range. It provided fine grazing for cattle and sheep. So cattle breeders set up large farms known as ranches. The great days of ranching were roughly between 1860 and 1890.

During that period, settlers were still moving westward, pushing back the frontier little by little. By 1890 the frontier had ceased to exist, and railroads had been built across the continent.

The men who herded the cattle on the range were known as cowboys. Each ranch had its own cattle, which were marked with a distinctive brand, such as the initials of the owner. When it came time to send the cattle to market, the cowboys from each ranch would ride out on the range to round up their own animals. Then the cattle would be driven to the nearest railroad depot.

Life was rough and tough. Cow-

▲ *Sir Walter Raleigh, English adventurer and writer.*

Walter Raleigh spelled his name "Rawley" or "Rawleyghe" up to 1584. After that date he always spelled it "Ralegh." He never spelled it Raleigh as most people do today.

▼ *Cowhands on ranches on the pampas of South America are called* gauchos. *The cattle are taken to markets such as this one in Mendoza, Argentina.*

▲ *Jeannette Rankin, the first woman elected to the U.S. Congress.*

▲ The Holy Family, *by the Italian painter Raphael.*

boys carried guns to fight off rustlers (cattle thieves). These guns were later used in bloody range wars when sheep farmers and homesteaders (small farmers) began competing for and fencing in the open land of the range.

Ranching is still carried on today, but there is much less open range for the cattle to run on. Cowboys, now generally called cowhands, still use horses for some of the rougher parts of the range, but they also use jeeps and trucks to get around. The bigger ranches often have their own helicopters. The raising of beef cattle is big business, and ranchers plant special grasses and use improved breeds of cattle to increase production.

ALSO READ: CATTLE, COWBOY, GREAT PLAINS.

RANKIN, JEANNETTE (1880–1973) The first woman to be elected to the U.S. Congress and one of the most prominent campaigners for women's rights in the United States was Jeannette Rankin. She was born on June 11, 1880 near Missoula in Montana. After attending college, she took up social work in Seattle, Washington, and became active in the struggle for women's suffrage (the right to vote and to hold public office).

In 1916, Jeannette Rankin was elected to the U.S. House of Representatives. She did not believe the United States should take part in World War I and spoke against it. This pacifist stance lost her the Republican Senate nomination in 1918. She ran as an independent but lost the election.

She returned to social work but was reelected to the House of Representatives in 1940. She voted against the U.S. declaration of war on Japan, and this virtually ended her career in politics. In the 1960's she started a women's cooperative homestead in

Georgia, and in 1968, at the age of 87, she led a women's protest against the Vietnam War.

ALSO READ: WOMEN'S RIGHTS.

RAPHAEL (1483–1520) One of the greatest painters of the Renaissance was Raphael (whose name in Italian is Raffaello Sanzio). Raphael was born in the northern Italian town of Urbino, where his father was the court painter for the Duke of Urbino. At the age of 21, Raphael went to Florence, where he studied the works of three great artists—Michelangelo, Leonardo da Vinci, and Fra Bartolommeo. He soon learned their techniques for showing light and shade and for painting dramatic action. Raphael showed an understanding of the structure of the human figure. Without copying their paintings, he was able to use their techniques in his own works. Learning to use others' ideas for his own purposes was one of Raphael's great talents.

At age 25, he was called to Rome by Pope Julius II to paint frescoes in four small rooms of the Vatican. He did a variety of paintings there, one of which was *School of Athens*. (See this painting in the article on DIMENSION.) In this picture, you can see poses and gestures Raphael borrowed from Michelangelo's works. The architectural background and use of perspective are like those Leonardo da Vinci used in the *Last Supper*. But the result is Raphael's own work—a very great painting.

Raphael's job at the Vatican became more important after a few years. He eventually had 50 painters working for him, and later he was made chief architect of St. Peter's Basilica (church) at the Vatican.

Shown here is one of many paintings Raphael did of the Holy Family. If you study the way the picture is planned, you will see why Raphael is considered a master of composition.

The Madonna is the center of attraction, yet the eyes of everyone in the painting are on the child Jesus. St. John looks at Jesus from one side, and Joseph looks on from the other. The placement of Mary's arm moves your eye up to Joseph to bring him into the composition.

ALSO READ: LEONARDO DA VINCI, MICHELANGELO, RENAISSANCE.

RAPID TRANSIT SYSTEM see RAILROAD, SUBWAY.

RARE ANIMAL An animal may be rare because it is *endangered*—it is in danger of dying out—or because it is *ecologically restricted*—it can only live in a very few places. We usually say that an animal is endangered if its numbers are getting smaller—if more of the animals are dying than are being born, or if the animals are fewer now than they were in the past. Ecologically restricted animals are not always endangered, but they are always in danger of being so. If their homes are destroyed, they cannot usually go anywhere else. And since there are only a few of them, they can die out very quickly.

It is not unusual for an animal to die out or become *extinct*. Of all the animal species (kinds) that ever lived, only a tiny handful survives today. Often when a species died out in the past, a new and different species arose and took its place. The total number of species was not reduced—the animal kingdom was as rich as before.

But what is happening today is that species are dying out, and they are all being replaced by only one species—human beings. A world with fewer animals is a poorer world, for us.

Human beings kill other animals in two ways. The first way is simple killing—animals are slaughtered for their fur or meat, or because they are a nuisance, or just for fun. The sec-

SOME RARE AND DEPLETED SPECIES

Animal	Distribution
Columbian white-tailed deer	Northwestern United States
Gray wolf	North America
Red kangaroo	Australia
Polar bear	Arctic regions
Giant panda	Tibet
Atlantic walrus	Northwestern Atlantic and Arctic Ocean
Black rhinoceros	Africa
Asiatic buffalo	Warmer countries of Asia
California gray whale	North Pacific
Bald eagle	North America
Peregrine falcon	Found in many parts of the world
Fin whale	Found in all oceans
West Indian manatee	West Indies and Central America
Leopard	Southern Asia and Africa
Ross seal	Antarctica
Pygmy hippopotamus	Liberia in Africa
California condor	Western United States
Mexican duck	Rio Grande Valley in Mexico
Galápagos flightless cormorant	Galápagos Islands
Whooping crane	North America
Desert tortoise	Western United States
Nilotic crocodile	Africa
Green turtle	Found in warm seas
Loggerhead turtle	Found in warm parts of the Atlantic Ocean

ond way is ecological destruction—destroying the places where animals live and the foods they eat, and disrupting the way they live. People also kill people, of course, and may soon find that they have endangered themselves.

Whales have been killed for their meat, for their oil, and for whalebone to make women's corsets. In the 1800's, millions of blue whales, white (or beluga) whales, and sperm whales roamed the sea. Since then, millions have been destroyed and all of these species are endangered. Laws have been passed to protect whales, but whalers (whale hunters) still kill thousands every year.

The prairie dog is a nuisance to farmers and ranchers because it eats crops and the grasses that cattle feed on. Millions of prairie dogs have been killed, and their numbers have been sharply reduced.

A great many animals have been killed, not for their fur or meat, or because they bother anyone, but just

▲ *A bald eagle. This bird, the official emblem of the United States, is now a rare animal. Many have been killed by farmers and ranchers as well as by pollution.*

▲ The North American buffalo or bison was hunted almost to extinction in the last century.

▲ American alligators were once hunted for their hide. Now, they are being killed off by water pollution.

▼ The sea otter was almost wiped out for its beautiful fur. It is now protected.

▲ The Californian condor, largest American bird of prey, has been hunted nearly to extinction.

▲ The rock fowl lives in West African forests. But the forests are rapidly being felled.

▼ The Caspian tiger was once common in the northern forests of Iran but may now be completely extinct in the wild.

▲ The Spanish lynx is fast disappearing because of gun-toting hunters and poisoned bait left by farmers.

▲ The Spanish eagle is another noble bird of prey threatened by farmers and hunters.

◄ The Komodo dragon is the world's largest living lizard—but it is under threat.

▼ The thylacine, or Tasmanian wolf, of Australia, is believed to be extinct, though sightings have been claimed.

because some people enjoy killing them. In the 1500's, Portuguese sailors clubbed to death the thousands of clumsy flightless dodo birds living on the island of Mauritius. More recently, the whooping crane and the sea otter have been almost completely killed off by hunters.

Mountain gorillas are the biggest and strongest of human relatives. But they are also rather quiet and lazy vegetarians (plant eaters) and will not bother any animal that does not bother them. In the push to develop Africa, people have destroyed many of the areas where gorillas live and have driven them into more crowded or less suitable places. The mountain gorilla is in danger of dying out because it cannot adapt to these new living places.

Peregrine falcons are fast flyers and clever hunters. They would appear to be natural survivors. But their numbers have decreased, which happened in a very strange way. Many farmers sprayed their crops with DDT, a powerful insecticide. Small animals ate the crops and swallowed the DDT. The peregrine falcons ate the animals and got the DDT into their own systems. The DDT weakened the shells of the eggs the falcons laid. The eggshells cracked before the young falcons were ready to hatch, and they died. Peregrine falcons thus became rare.

If we don't want rare animals to become extinct animals, we must protect them. Laws must be passed to stop the intentional killing of endangered animals. The animals' natural homes must be preserved (saved), and protected areas must be set aside for animals whose natural home sites have been destroyed.

Today there are national and international agencies, such as the World Wildlife Fund and Greenpeace, that focus attention on the plight of endangered species. They lobby governments to pass conservation legislation and encourage international coopera-tion in controlling such activities as whaling and seal slaughter. Many countries have passed laws controlling the commercial import and export of animals.

Animals can take care of themselves if they are left alone. On a few small islands off New Zealand live lizardlike reptiles called tuataras. They are gentle, lazy animals that take 20 years to become adults. They would be prime candidates for extinction if they had any enemies or if more ambitious animals lived nearby. But about their only neighbors on the island are petrels—seabirds—and the petrels share their nests with the tuataras. Living in peace and quiet, the tuatara has not changed in 200 million years. Only recently, when people began hunting it for its meat and hide, was the tuatara in any danger. But now it is protected by law. The tuatara is ecologically restricted, and it is rare, but fortunately it is not endangered.

ALSO READ: BIRDS OF THE PAST, ECOLOGY, EVOLUTION, MAMMALS OF THE PAST, WHALES AND WHALING.

RARE-EARTH ELEMENTS see ELEMENT.

RATS AND MICE Rats and mice that originally came from the Old World belong to the family of rodents called *Muridae*. Rats and mice native to the Americas are in a different rodent family, *Cricetidae*. All these rodents are alike in certain ways. Rats are usually bigger than mice, but both animals are furry, with long hairless tails and pointed ears and snouts. Both can be house vermin (destructive pests).

Rats There were no rats in North and South America before the Europeans arrived. Rats from the colonists' ships came ashore and began to

The rarest mammal is probably the Tasmanian wolf or thylacine. This marsupial has a head like a dog and hind quarters rather like a kangaroo. The animals were once numerous in Australia but have been almost certainly wiped out. A few sightings have been claimed in Tasmania.

▼ *The house mouse is attracted to homes where there are food supplies such as in pantries and kitchen cabinets.*

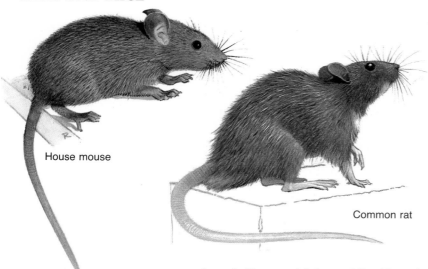

House mouse

Common rat

▲ *Two well-known members of the rat and mouse family. The house mouse and common rat are considered pests, as they are a health hazard and can spread disease.*

▼ *The black rat, an early immigrant to the United States, is a less aggressive relative of the brown rat.*

breed. Rats multiply rapidly. Female rats begin breeding when only five months old. They give birth to litters of from 8 to 14 ratlings about five times a year. Rats are usually *nocturnal*, doing most of their foraging for food at night and sleeping by day.

Rats have many habits and other characteristics in common with human beings. Rats can eat a great variety of food, as do people. Rats can live in many different environments—forests, deserts, mountains, and cities—as people do. Rats are subject to many of the same diseases that people contract. Rats are aggressive and will fight and kill their own kind, just as human beings do. Most other mammals will not kill their own kind.

The two most common types of rat are the *brown rat* (sometimes called the *Norway rat*) and the *black rat*. The brown rat is larger and bolder than the black rat. It has grayish-brown fur and measures about 16 inches (40 cm) in length, including its 7½-inch-long (19-cm-long) tail. The brown rat lives underground—in burrows, sewers, cellars, subways, and under houses and barns. The brown rat is a pest, attacking crops, domestic animals, and sometimes people.

The black rat is only about half as large as the brown rat and is less aggressive. The black rat was brought to the United States aboard ships in about the 1500's. The brown rat was brought in later and has driven the

black rat out of many areas. Most black rats now live in tropical and subtropical climates.

Both the black and brown rat are harmful to human beings. They eat and spoil food in warehouses and on farms. They carry diseases, such as typhus fever and bubonic plague, that are dangerous to people. Because rats and people have so much in common, the *albino* (white strains) of both brown and black rats are bred for scientific study. By using rats, scientists are able to run tests on diet, medicines, diseases, growth, heredity, learning processes, and many other factors. Experimentation on rats helps scientists make discoveries that will aid people.

Other varieties of rat include the *roof rat*, a type of black rat that has migrated from Egypt to other warm areas of the world. The *bush* or *wood rats* are edible. They live far from human habitation in forests and deserts. They eat only plants. The *pack rat* of the South Atlantic coast and the coast of the Gulf of Mexico collects objects—especially shiny ones—in its burrow. The *bushy-tailed wood rat* lives west of the Rocky Mountains and has a very furry tail.

Mice Like rats, mice are found in great numbers throughout the world. They, too, can live in many different environments. Female mice breed every 10 to 17 weeks all year round. They have from five to ten young in each litter. Mice are harmful to people in much the same way as rats are. Albino mice are also used in scientific experiments.

There are hundreds of varieties of mice. Perhaps the best-known mouse is the common *house mouse*. This furry little creature lives in buildings, as well as in fields and forests. House mice that live outdoors are about 6½ inches (17 cm) long, including their tails. They eat insects and the roots, leaves, and seeds of plants. Outdoor house mice usually come out only at night. House mice that live in buildings are slightly larger than those living outdoors because they are usually better fed. They like everything from ice cream and beer to soap and paste.

House mice are yellowish gray on top, often streaked with black, with a lighter gray underneath. Outdoor house mice build underground nests which they line with grass. Indoor house mice build nests in attics, basements, and inside walls, also lining them with soft materials.

Other varieties of mice include the *white-footed mouse*, which is slightly larger than the house mouse and has four white patches on its feet. The *cotton mouse* is found in the southern United States where it damages cotton crops by feeding on the plants and seedlings. The *grasshopper mouse* of the western states feeds almost entirely on insects and spiders. The *field mouse* is not really a mouse at all. It is a *vole*—a type of rodent that looks like a mouse but has a shorter tail. The *pocket mouse* is not a mouse either. It belongs to a genus of rodents that have fur-lined cheek pouches.

ALSO READ: ANIMAL, ANIMAL DISTRIBUTION, ANIMAL HOMES, MAMMAL, PET, RODENT.

READING   see LITERACY.

REAGAN, RONALD WILSON (born 1911) The U.S. Presidential election in 1980 was won by Ronald Reagan, a conservative Republican. A strong tide of conservatism throughout the United States helped him defeat Jimmy Carter, the Democratic candidate. At the same time, many influential Democratic members of Congress were swept out of office. Reagan's running mate, George Bush, was elected Vice-President.

Reagan was born in Tampico, Illinois. After graduating from college, he worked as a radio sportscaster for five years. At that time, he was a liberal Democrat who supported President Franklin Roosevelt. From 1937 to 1966, Reagan worked as an actor in movies and on television. He was a U.S. Army officer during World War II. Reagan headed the Screen Actors Guild and the Motion Picture Industry Council in the 1940's and 1950's.

His politics gradually became conservative, and in 1962, Reagan formally declared himself a Republican. He was elected governor of California in 1966 and was reelected in 1970. Many business leaders supported Reagan, who advocated government spending cuts.

Upon becoming President, Reagan sought to fulfill his campaign prom-

When Ronald Reagan became President in 1981 he was the oldest person ever to be inaugurated. He was 69. William Henry Harrison was 68 when he was inaugurated in 1841. The youngest President at inauguration was Theodore Roosevelt. He was 42.

President Reagan was the first President to claim Illinois as his native state. There have been eight Presidents from Virginia and seven from Ohio.

RONALD WILSON REAGAN
FORTIETH PRESIDENT   JANUARY 20, 1981–JANUARY 20, 1989

Born: February 6, 1911, Tampico, Illinois
Parents: John Edward and Nellie Wilson Reagan
Education: Eureka College, Eureka, Illinois
Religion: Christian Church (Disciples of Christ)
Occupation: Actor and politician
State Represented: California
Political Party: Republican
Married: 1940 to Jane Wyman (born 1914) Divorced, 1948
1952 to Nancy Davis (born 1923)
Children: 1 daughter, 1 son (adopted) by first wife
1 daughter, 1 son by second wife

▲ The Sower, *by the French painter, Jean François Millet.*

▼ Beach in Normandy, *by Gustave Courbet. National Gallery of Art, Washington, D.C., Chester Dale Collection.*

ises. Government programs were reduced, and tax cuts were passed by Congress. Reagan sought to balance the budget and to strengthen U.S. military defense. He fired striking air traffic controllers and appointed the first woman to the U.S. Supreme Court. An attempt to assassinate Reagan failed in 1981. In 1987 Reagan signed an historic treaty with Soviet leader Mikhail Gorbachev. The U.S.–U.S.S.R. pact aimed to reduce the storehouse of nuclear arms.

ALSO READ: CARTER, JAMES EARL, JR.

REALISM Many artists in the mid-1800's were painting pictures of imaginary people and places. This trend, called Romanticism, did not suit a French artist named Gustave Courbet. Courbet felt that artists should paint not imaginary scenes but real scenes of real life. Courbet therefore began to paint in what is called a realistic manner. In 1849, he painted *The Stone Breakers*. This painting (destroyed in World War II) showed the backs of two men hard at work breaking stone. It was a truthful scene—not one of romantic fantasy.

Courbet had a one-man show of his paintings in a shack in Paris in 1855. He called the exhibition "Realism, G. Courbet." Truth was what he was looking for in painting. He felt that truth lay in Realism—painting life the way it really was.

Shown on this page is a landscape by Courbet, *Beach in Normandy*. This scene is not idealized (made to seem perfect and beautiful) as the Romantics would have had it. The tide is out, and the boats sit beached until high tide comes to take them away. A Romantic painter would have put in a sunset, brought in the tide, or perhaps even changed the boats into large ships or barks of a mythological character.

Another painter who turned to painting everyday life was Jean François Millet. He liked painting figures. He wanted to show the poor peasants in the fields as they really looked. His idea was rather shocking because at this time most artists painted rich people gracefully posed. Look at his painting shown here, *The Sower*. The sower moves deliberately with a steady rhythm sowing the field, while the birds fly behind, looking for any seed they might pick up. Millet does not make the sower look elegant but like a solid, hard-working French peasant. You can see that Millet respected sowing as an important action. But he does not try to make it romantic or pretty. He makes it seem true to life. Millet made painters aware of the beauty of common people doing everyday tasks. In a way, Realism paved the way for Impressionism, the movement in which artists became even more aware of everyday scenes and the light and the weather at various times of day.

ALSO READ: IMPRESSIONISM, ROMANTIC PERIOD.

RECIPE see COOKING.

RECONSTRUCTION The effort made by Congress between 1865 and 1877 to rebuild the war-torn South just after the Civil War is called the period of Reconstruction. The defeated South had many problems. Cities and farms had been destroyed or badly damaged. There was little food or money. State and local governments were in a confused condition.

The Civil War had freed the black people. They were no longer slaves who could be owned and treated like a piece of property. Freedmen (as ex-slaves were then called) needed land, money, and education to get started in their new roles as free citizens. But former slaves had none of these things. They could not even serve on juries, testify in court, or vote—the basic rights of any U.S. citizen. If black people were to survive as freedmen, help had to come from the North. The black people's first problem was to get white Southerners to accept them as a free people.

The Legacy of War During the Civil War, eleven Southern states had split off from the United States. They had formed a separate nation, calling themselves the Confederate States of America. After the war, some Northern members of Congress felt that Southerners should be punished for having left the Union. President Lincoln and his successor, President Andrew Johnson, felt that the Confederate States should be welcomed back into the Union with as little bitterness as possible. They decided that the Confederate States should be helped in reconstructing (rebuilding) their lands and governments. These Presidents also declared that freedmen must be ensured of their rights as individuals.

The Proclamation of Amnesty and Reconstruction was issued by President Lincoln in 1863, in the midst of the war. He offered pardon to Confederate people who would promise to support the Constitution. The Confederate States could reenter the Union as soon as one-tenth of their voters had made this promise and set

up a state government. After the war, Northern members of Congress set even stricter terms for the reentry of Southern states into the Union. Every Confederate state had to ratify (approve) the newly written Thirteenth, Fourteenth, and Fifteenth amendments to the Constitution. The Thirteenth Amendment declared slavery illegal in the United States. The Fourteenth Amendment gave blacks full rights as free citizens. The Fifteenth Amendment gave all male citizens the right to vote.

Southern legislators refused to ratify the new amendments. White political leaders especially disliked the Fourteenth and Fifteenth amendments. All kinds of ways were devised to keep freedmen from voting, holding office, or otherwise using their citizenship rights. Southern whites voted each other into office.

When the thirty-ninth Congress met in Washington in December 1865, representatives and senators from the South included the vice-president of the former Confederate States, four Confederate generals, five Confederate colonels, six members of the Confederate cabinet, and 58 members of the Confederate States Congress. None of these persons had approved the Constitutional amendments, and none was in sympathy with citizenship for black people. These former Confederates were not allowed seats in Congress and so returned home to take charge at state

▲ *During the period of Reconstruction, many black people were elected to political office in the South. Hiram R. Revels (left) from Mississippi was the first black U.S. Senator. Here he is shown with U.S. representatives (second from left to right) Benjamin Turner of Alabama, Robert DeLarge of South Carolina, Josiah Walls of Florida, Jefferson Long of Georgia, and Joseph Rainy and Robert Brown Elliot of South Carolina.*

One of the most frightening organizations to spring up during the Reconstruction period was the Ku Klux Klan. It began at Pulaski, Tennessee, in 1866 and soon spread throughout the South. Members of the Klan draped themselves and their horses in white sheets and rode around at night killing and terrifying blacks and people who sympathized with them. Remnants of the Klan still exist.

▲ *This Freedmen's Bureau primary school in Vicksburg, Mississippi, was set up to provide former slaves with an education so that they could qualify for better jobs and could exercise their full citizenship rights.*

▶ *This cartoon depicts a "carpetbagger." The term was used to describe Northern adventurers seeking fortune and political power in the defeated Southern states in the period called Reconstruction, after the Civil War. They carried their possessions in carpetbags. Many carpetbaggers were in fact honest people who went south to help build up the crippled states' economy, education, and administration.*

and local levels. There they passed laws that limited the rights of former slaves. Blacks could not testify in court and could not travel without a permit. Blacks who had no jobs were arrested and made to pay a large fine. If unable to pay, blacks were handed over to employers who paid the fine and then forced blacks to work for them. In this way, thousands of blacks were forced into a new kind of slavery.

The Freedmen's Bureau On March 3, 1865, the Freedmen's Bureau was established. The bureau's job included the feeding and clothing of war refugees. The bureau set up schools for blacks and supplied medical services for all in need. It managed lands and other property that were deserted by or taken from Confederates during the war. One of the bureau's most important jobs was to supervise contracts between freedmen and their white employers (who were often the blacks' former masters).

To make sure Southern states accepted the new Constitutional amendments, Congress passed the Reconstruction Act of 1867. This law divided the former Confederate States into five military districts, each governed by a Northern army commander. Thousands of black voters, supported and defended by U.S.

troops, went to the polls and began voting former Confederates out of state and local offices. New officials took their places. Some were dishonest white Northerners, called *carpetbaggers*, who came to the South to make money out of the mixed-up conditions. Some were white Southerners, called *scalawags*, who sided with the North. But many of these new officials were black people. They ranged from highly educated to the poor and illiterate (unable to read or write). Some were cautious officials, and some were bold and daring. Some felt sorry for the defeated Confederates, and others were angry and bitter. These new black leaders were elected to state and local governments and to the U.S. Congress.

From 1867 to 1877, Reconstruction legislatures made great changes in the laws. They wrote new state constitutions, ensuring civil rights for all, that lasted for many years. They did away with laws that sent people to jail because they owed money. They established free public schools for everyone, and they ratified the three new amendments to the Constitution. But the accomplishments of these legislatures were drowned out by white Confederates who accused black leaders of corruption (illegal dealings). These charges had a terrible effect, because people began to believe them. Some black officials *were* corrupt—but so were many whites. The North was getting tired of spending money and sympathy on the "Southern problem" that seemed never to end. White Southerners, who had been used to low taxes before the war, were furious at being taxed by black legislators to provide money for schools and new roads.

White Power Restored By 1869, former Confederate officials, white landowners, and out-of-work politicians were determined to regain control of their states, even if it meant working with poor whites, called *red-*

necks. The idea was to use any way possible—from speeches to murder—to restore white power. Black citizens began to be attacked by terrorist gangs of night-riders, such as the Ku Klux Klan, the Knights of the White Camellia, and the Red Shirts. They whipped and murdered blacks and any whites who supported civil rights for blacks.

Soon, black people were defeated in elections or forced out of office by white terrorist groups. White Confederates took control of North Carolina in 1870, Texas in 1873, Arkansas and Alabama in 1874, Mississippi in 1875, South Carolina in 1876, and Florida and Louisiana in 1877. They had already expelled blacks from the Georgia legislature (1868) and taken control of Tennessee in 1869.

The Presidential election of 1876 killed once and for all the hopes of Southern blacks for equality. Samuel Tilden (the Democratic candidate favored by Southern whites) ran against the Republican, Rutherford B. Hayes. When votes were counted, a dispute arose over the number of votes cast in Oregon, Louisiana, Florida, and South Carolina. Republican leaders and Southern officials agreed to give the election to Hayes. But it is thought that Southern leaders agreed to accept Hayes if he would, as President, give the South financial aid. In order to get Hayes elected, Republicans also agreed to withdraw the last federal troops from the South.

As the troops disappeared, so did any further attempts at Reconstruction. The hopes of freed black people for civil rights, schools, paying jobs, and real dignity were silenced for almost 100 years.

ALSO READ: AMERICAN HISTORY; BLACK AMERICANS; CIVIL RIGHTS; CIVIL RIGHTS MOVEMENT; CIVIL WAR; CONFEDERATE STATES OF AMERICA; CONSTITUTION, UNITED STATES; HAYES, RUTHERFORD B.; JOHNSON, ANDREW; LINCOLN, ABRAHAM.

RECORDING If you love music, you can listen to your favorite tunes or songs wherever you are. You can have a disc or cassette player at home and in the car, or you can carry your own personal player with you. You can listen to music on the telephone. All this wealth of music is made possible by sound recording. In addition, most of the music you can hear on the radio and television is music that has been recorded. A video is a recording of vision, as in television pictures, as well as of sound.

Thomas Alva Edison invented sound recording in 1877. He built the first phonograph, which played wax cylinders with grooves like those on an LP or single record. The record player is a direct descendant of Edison's phonograph. However, like other kinds of players, it produces sound in a different way.

How Sound Recording Works
There are several different systems for recording sound, but they all work in the same general way. First, a microphone changes the sound waves in speech, song, or music into electric signals. These audio or sound signals are then stored on a tape or disc. When the tape or disc is played, the player produces the electric signals again.

▲ *In a recording studio, the producer and engineer sit at the mixing console. They listen to the orchestra (seen through the soundproof window) through loudspeakers. The sounds are monitored at the console and then fed to the tape-recording machine.*

Crystals such as quartz behave in an interesting way. If an alternating electric current is passed through them, they vibrate in time with the changing flow of the current. This effect is used to make very accurate clocks and to keep broadcasting transmitters at exactly the right frequency.
The effect works the other way, too. If these crystals (called piezoelectric) are made to vibrate very quickly, they produce an electric current of that frequency. It is crystals such as these that are used in phonograph pickups to change the vibrations of the needle in the record groove into electric current for the amplifier.

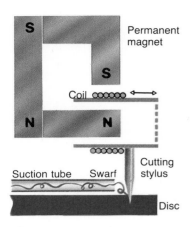

▲ *Parts of an electric cutting head for making record discs. The coil is attracted and repelled by the permanent magnet according to the strength of the sound signal, which varies the groove cut by the stylus.*

▲ *Making cassette tapes is a major industry. Top: large rolls of tape are polished. The tape is then coated with iron oxide and stored (center). At bottom, the coated tape is slit into cassette width, 0.15 inches (3.8 mm).*

They go to an amplifier, which makes the signals stronger so that they can travel along wires and power a loudspeaker or earphones.

In recording, the sound signals are stored in four different ways. On LP or single records, the signals are stored as the wiggles in the groove on the surface of the record. On a compact disc, the signals are in the form of patterns of tiny holes in the surface. On tape cassettes and reels of tape, the sound signals are stored as magnetic patterns in a magnetic coating on the tape. The sound in a motion picture is recorded as light and dark patterns in a track at the side of the film.

A complete stereo system has all the equipment you need to play any recording that you can buy. It has a record player to play LP and single records, one or two tape players to play back tape cassettes and to record sounds on tape, a compact disc player, a radio, an amplifier, and two loudspeakers, plus an earphone connection. It may also have a graphic equalizer, which allows you to alter the tone of the sounds.

Tape Recording   In a recording studio, singers and musicians record their music on a large tape recorder. This is like a cassette player but uses big reels of tape. Each microphone sends an electric signal to the tape recorder. The record head in the tape recorder contains an electromagnet that converts the electric signal into a magnetic field that varies in strength. The magnetic tape moves past the record head. In the surface of the tape are millions of tiny metal particles. The magnetic field magnetizes the particles so that the electric sound signal is stored on the tape as a magnetic pattern. The tape recorder also has a replay head, which converts the magnetic pattern back into an electric sound signal as the tape moves past it.

A big tape recorder used in a recording studio has as many as 24

▲ *Mahalia Jackson goes over the music for a song she is about to record with Duke Ellington and his orchestra. Miss Jackson died in 1972, but her great gospel singing lives on in the records she made.*

record heads and 24 replay heads. It can record the sound signals from 24 microphones or electronic instruments such as synthesizers in 24 separate tracks on the tape. The tape is then used to make a master tape. All the signals from the big recorder are mixed together to make a master tape. This has only two tracks—one each for the two loudspeakers in a stereo player. Records, compact discs, and cassette tapes are then made from this master tape, or the master tape may be broadcast over the radio.

A tape player uses tape cassettes. These have four tracks—two going one way and two the other so that the cassette has stereo music on both sides. There is usually just one head that records or replays. An erase head wipes out an old recording before a new one is made. It produces a magnetic field that removes any magnetic pattern from the tape.

Records   When a record is made, the electric signals from the master tape go to a machine which cuts a wiggly groove in a master disc. The disc spins at 33⅓ or 45 rpm (revolutions per minute). The records that people buy are copies of this disc.

When a record is played, a needle or stylus is placed in the groove. As the record spins, the stylus vibrates.

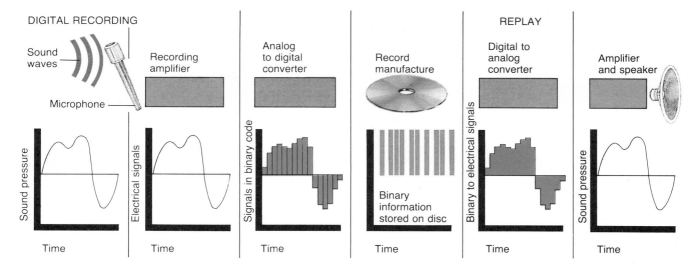

DIGITAL RECORDING

Sound waves

Microphone

Recording amplifier

Analog to digital converter

Record manufacture

Binary information stored on disc

REPLAY

Digital to analog converter

Amplifier and speaker

Sound pressure — Time

Electrical signals — Time

Signals in binary code — Time

Time

Binary to electrical signals — Time

Sound pressure — Time

A pickup (cartridge) attached to the stylus produces the electric signals that then go to an amplifier.

Compact discs When a compact disc is made, the electric signals from the master tape go to a machine containing a laser. They cause the laser beam to flash on and off extremely quickly, and the laser burns a spiral track of millions of minute holes in a spinning disc.

Analog and Digital There are two basic kinds of ways in which sound is recorded—analog and digital. Records are analog, compact discs are digital, and tapes may be either analog or digital. Digital is better.

In digital recording, a computer measures the changing voltage of the electric sound signal from the microphone thousands of times a second. It converts the measurements into code numbers. In the player, a computer changes the code numbers back into an electric sound signal.

In analog recording, the recording—a wiggly groove or magnetic pattern—is a direct copy of the electric sound signal in another form. As the voltage changes, the groove or pattern changes too.

ALSO READ: EDISON, THOMAS ALVA; COMPACT DISCS; ELECTRONICS; FILM; MUSIC; SOUND; VIDEO.

RECYCLING see WASTE DISPOSAL.

RED CROSS A patient who needs blood in a New York hospital, and a victim of an earthquake in Iran may each be helped by the Red Cross. Caring *about* and caring *for* others are ideals shared by the International Committee of the Red Cross; the League of Red Cross Societies; and more than 120 national Red Cross, Red Crescent, Red Mogen David, and Red Lion and Sun societies—all of whom belong to the Red Cross.

In 1859, a Swiss banker named Jean Henri Dunant was very troubled by the suffering he saw by chance on a battlefield while on a trip to Italy. Dunant originated the idea of forming voluntary national societies for the care of ill and wounded soldiers dur-

Red Cross

Red Crescent

Red Lion and Sun

▲ *In the digital recording/ replay system, the signals from the microphone are changed into a series of digits in binary code. In this form, the signals are less prone to distortion, noise, and speed changes. To play the sounds, the signals are changed from digital back to analog.*

▲ *Jean Henri Dunant of Switzerland was the founder of the Red Cross.*

◄ *The Red Cross symbol and its Muslim counterpart, the Red Crescent. In Iran the Red Lion and Sun was chosen as a symbol because the people were followers of a different sect of Islam.*

The Red Sea is growing wider. Scientists believe that one day it will become a giant ocean.

▼ Looking toward Jordan from the Gulf of Aqaba in the Red Sea.

ing the war—no matter whose side they were fighting on. One result of Dunant's efforts was the Geneva Convention of 1864. This treaty between nations began the Red Cross movement. Today, wounded and sick, prisoners of war, and civilians are all under the protection of the Geneva Convention.

In 1881, Clara Barton began the organization now known as the American Red Cross (ARC).

ALSO READ: BARTON, CLARA; FIRST AID.

RED SEA The Red Sea is a body of water that is almost closed in by land. It separates the Arabian peninsula and northeastern Africa.

The Red Sea lies between the sandy shores of Saudi Arabia on the east, and Egypt, Sudan, and Ethiopia on the west. At its southern end, the Red Sea reaches the Gulf of Aden and the Arabian Sea through a narrow channel. (See the map with the article on the MIDDLE EAST.)

At its northern end, the Red Sea branches in two directions, separated by the Sinai Peninsula. The Gulf of Aqaba leads to the Israeli port of Elath. The Gulf of Suez leads to the Suez Canal. When the canal opened in 1869, ships could then sail from Asia to Europe through the Mediterranean, making the extremely long voyage around Africa unnecessary.

The Red Sea is about 1,400 miles (2,250 km) long and up to 220 miles (355 km) wide. Its waters fill part of a large crack in the Earth's surface called the Great Rift. The Red Sea is more than 7,000 feet (2,135 m) deep in spots. Ship captains must navigate carefully to avoid large, dangerous coral reefs.

The sea may have received its name from the reddish algae that cover the surface of the water in some places and make the water look red.

The Bible tells of Moses leading the Israelites through the Red Sea. Scholars believe that the Bible writer meant the "Sea of Reeds," a marshy area at the tip of the Gulf of Suez. Moses could have guided his followers on foot through this sea of reeds, but the pursuing Egyptian chariots would have bogged down in the swamp.

ALSO READ: SUEZ CANAL.

REED, WALTER (1851–1902) Walter Reed was an American doctor who discovered the cause of yellow fever and demonstrated how it could be controlled.

Walter Reed was born in Gloucester County, Virginia. He joined the United States Army Medical Corps in 1875. In 1893, he was made a professor at the Army Medical College in Washington, D.C.

The Spanish-American War broke out in 1898. Many American soldiers sent to Cuba to fight in the war were dying of typhoid fever and yellow fever. Reed thought that flies and dust were the cause of the spread of typhoid fever. He recommended the camps be cleaned up.

When this proved successful, Reed was put in charge of a group of doctors who were in Cuba trying to find ways to control yellow fever. Reed thought that the disease was carried by the bite of a mosquito. Several doctors who belonged to Reed's group and a few soldier volunteers allowed themselves to be bitten by mosquitoes that had bitten persons sick with yellow fever. The volunteers soon became ill with the disease. Two of them died as a result. But the test proved that mosquitoes were the carriers of yellow fever. As a result of Walter Reed's work, the mosquitoes have been controlled and yellow fever has nearly been wiped out. One of Reed's assistants, William Crawford Gorgas, took Reed's discoveries to the Panama Canal Zone. He got rid of yellow fever there and made possible the digging of the Panama Canal.

ALSO READ: DISEASE, MEDICINE, MOSQUITO, SPANISH-AMERICAN WAR.

REED INSTRUMENTS see WOODWIND INSTRUMENTS.

REFERENCE BOOK
Nearly every home has a dictionary and a cookbook—two of the most common kinds of reference books. Reference books are collections of information arranged (often in alphabetical order) so that a reader can easily refer to them to find the specific information he or she is searching for.

General Reference Books General reference books are filled with information on many subjects. *Dictionaries* contain lists of words with their pronunciations, meanings, and origins. A *thesaurus* gives a list of words and with them, those words that have the same, similar, and opposite meanings. A thesaurus is useful when you cannot think of precisely the word you need. General reference *encyclopedias* contain articles summarizing information in almost every field of study. An *atlas* is a collection of maps of a city, a country, or the world.

A *bibliography* is a reference book about other books. It contains lists of books and articles that provide infor-

mation on a particular subject. Yearbooks, or *almanacs*, are published annually and contain important world information of the previous year. You can find in an almanac such varied information as the height of a mountain or the number of touchdowns scored by a certain team last year.

Specialized Reference Books Some reference books provide information on more specialized subjects. Foreign-language dictionaries give pronunciations and translate words from one language to another. Many dictionaries are even more specialized and provide meanings only for words in a particular field, such as music or mythology. Some encyclopedias contain articles on only one subject, such as astronomy. *Handbooks* and *guides* usually provide instruction in a certain activity, such as fishing, or information about a specific subject or place. Information about local, state, and federal governments is often given in *manuals*, *registers*, and *directories*. Certain reference books consist of brief biographies of famous people. For example, *Who's Who in America* contains biographies of well-known living Americans.

The Reference Section Libraries contain areas devoted to reference

▲ *Walter Reed, U.S. Army Medical Corps doctor.*

▼ *A gathering of intellectuals in Paris in the 1750's that included Diderot, the French writer and philosopher who compiled the first great encyclopedia. It was called simply the* Encyclopédie, *and took Diderot 20 years to produce.*

▲ *These pupils are learning to use a reference library, an important skill that will be useful in their studies later on.*

books. The reference section in a library is often in a separate room. The reader cannot check out these books, so they will always be available for everyone to use.

Some libraries put a second copy of a popular nonfiction book, even a cookbook, in the reference section. The choice of books in the reference section usually reflects the needs and interests of the readers who use it.

ALSO READ: ALMANAC, ATLAS, BIBLIOGRAPHY, CARD CATALOG, DICTIONARY, ENCYCLOPEDIA, INDEX, LIBRARY, LIBRARY OF CONGRESS.

REFLECTION see LIGHT, MIRROR.

REFRIGERATION If you put some ice in an insulated chest full of warm food, the ice will slowly melt and the food will get colder. This happens because heat always moves from a warm body to a cold body. The heat in the warm food passes into the ice. This makes the ice warmer and causes it to melt. It makes the food colder because it now has less heat. This *transfer* (movement) of heat goes on until the ice has melted.

A refrigerator is more complicated than an ice chest, but it works the same way. In a refrigerator a liquid,

No one knows when it was discovered that liquids in porous pots keep cool if left in a wind. The liquid seeps through the pot and evaporates. During evaporation, energy is given off in the form of heat. Heat is therefore continually removed from the contents of the pot.

▶ *A refrigerator works by taking the heat from inside to the outside. A special fluid is pumped through pipes in the refrigerator to carry the heat out via an evaporator and condenser. Food and drink is kept at a cool temperature which can be controlled by a dial. (1) Control dial; (2) heat absorbed by evaporator; (3) heat given out by condenser; (4) pump.*

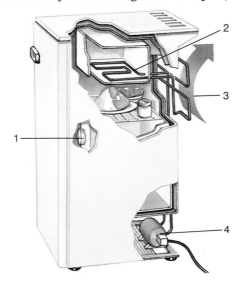

▲ *Refrigerated transport makes it possible to ship perishable foods fast and efficiently.*

called a *refrigerant*, does the work of the ice, absorbing heat from inside the refrigerator. The liquid refrigerant is evaporated in coils (metal tubes). As it evaporates, the refrigerant picks up the heat from inside the refrigerator. Then the refrigerant is put under high pressure so that it changes back to a liquid and gives off the heat to the outside air. The same refrigerant is reused.

A refrigerator has thick, insulated walls. Insulation prevents heat or cold from passing through a wall. A well-insulated refrigerator does not run all the time. It has a *thermostat*, a combination thermometer and switch, that turns on the refrigerator when it gets too warm.

Foods are refrigerated to keep them from spoiling. Many of the bacteria that can spoil food cannot grow at temperatures below 40° or 50° F (4.4° or 10° C). The maximum (highest) safe temperature for storing foods that can spoil is 50° F (10° C). Food preserved by freezing will stay fresh for longer periods. The temperature of a home freezer is usually about 0° F (−18° C).

ALSO READ: BACTERIA, FOOD, FOOD PROCESSING, GAS, HEAT AND COLD, LIQUID.

REFUGEE A refugee is a person who leaves his or her homeland to seek refuge, or shelter, in another country. A refugee often leaves to escape war or persecution. The term "refugee" also applies to people who have been left homeless because of war or natural disasters, such as earthquakes, famine, or floods. Refugees are considered refugees until they are reestablished in their own country or living permanently in a new country and able to earn a living.

Refugees and immigrants are similar, but there is one important difference. Immigrants leave their homeland of their own free will. Refugees are forced to leave.

It was not difficult for a refugee to find a new place to live until the 1900's. Since then, finding homes for refugees has become an international problem. The United Nations has set up a commission to help find homes for refugees from wars and revolutions. Refugees who can find no homes are often forced to live in refugee camps, where living conditions are difficult. More than a million Arab refugees from Palestine have lived in temporary camps in nearby lands since the Arab-Israeli War of 1948, when Palestine became Israel. The U.S. government has recently helped many refugees from Vietnam, Cuba, and Haiti. Since 1980, many refugees have faced starvation in war-torn Lebanon.

ALSO READ: IMMIGRATION, UNITED NATIONS.

REGENERATION If your hair is cut, it soon grows back. Your fingernails continue to grow as long as you live. Hair and fingernails replace themselves, or *regenerate*. Among many kinds of animals, regeneration includes the ability to replace whole parts of the body. A lizard that loses its tail can grow a new one. A lobster can regenerate a missing claw.

Among higher animals, most examples of regeneration are everyday events. Human beings and other mammals replace hair, skin, and claws. Birds grow new feathers at least once a year. Deer shed antlers and grow new ones. But human beings and other mammals cannot grow new limbs. Many lower animals can do this.

Salamanders can sometimes replace lost legs or tails. If a salamander loses its entire leg, or a part of it, the wound quickly heals. Then a knob of tissue begins growing. Within a few weeks a complete leg has replaced the lost one. In certain lower animals, a whole new individual sometimes grows out of one piece of the old body. One arm of a starfish, if it has a piece of the center, can regenerate a whole new body. The hydra is a freshwater polyp that regenerates from a tiny section of its old body. Regeneration takes place in common earthworms. Earthworms are divided into sections, or segments, that can usually grow back if cut away.

Certain animals get rid of body parts deliberately in order to save themselves from enemies. Then they regenerate the lost part. If you pick up a lizard by its tail, the animal may escape by leaving its tail in your hand and scurrying off without it. Many lower animals, such as starfish, crabs, and some insects, avoid capture by letting legs drop off.

ALSO READ: ANIMAL, GROWTH.

▲ *A refugee from the Korean War of 1950 to 1953. Civilians fleeing from war or natural disaster are often made refugees in their own countries.*

◀ *Some animals can regenerate (regrow) new limbs or other parts of their bodies. The starfish can replace a lost arm. What is even more extraordinary, a severed arm can grow four additional arms and develop into a complete animal.*

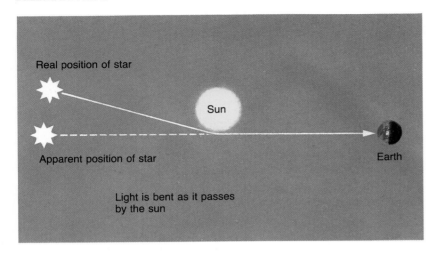

Real position of star

Sun

Apparent position of star

Earth

Light is bent as it passes
by the sun

▲ *Part of Einstein's theory of relativity concluded that the force of gravity distorts space. Then Einstein said that a strong field of gravity, such as that of the sun or a star, would bend light rays. This would affect the real position of heavenly bodies as observed from the Earth.*

Albert Einstein's theories of relativity produced some very astonishing conclusions. One of these was that things get heavier and time slows down as they move. The faster they move, the heavier they become. At the speed of light, mass would become infinite and time would stop. This means that no object, such as a spaceship, could travel at, or faster than, the speed of light.

RELATIVITY Imagine that you are standing by the side of a road and a car passes by going 30 miles (50 km) an hour. You judge the speed by imagining that you are at rest and the car is moving. (In fact you know that you are not really at rest, because the Earth on which you stand is turning and moving around the sun. The sun itself is moving through space.) This is the basic idea of relativity: assuming that you are not moving and working out the speed of something that is moving *relative* to you.

You can easily think of other examples. For instance, if you are moving in a car at 30 miles (50 km) an hour and another car is approaching you at 40 miles (65 km) an hour, it seems to be coming toward you at 70 miles (115 km) an hour. We say that the second car is moving 70 miles an hour relative to the first car.

Toward the end of the last century, some very surprising results appeared in experiments on the speed of light. It seems that this speed is always the same no matter how fast the source of light moves. It is always 186,000 miles (299,330 km) a second.

In 1905, Albert Einstein introduced a theory of relative motion to explain this strange fact. The first part dealt with observations made about things moving in a straight line at a constant speed. It was called the *special* theory of relativity. One of the

things Einstein assumed was that the speed of everything must be measured relative to the speed of light.

This may seem quite a simple idea in itself, but it had far-reaching effects on the ideas of science. Some implications were very strange. For instance, Einstein showed that the faster things move the more mass they have and the slower time seems to pass relative to time as measured by an outside observer. A person traveling in a fast-moving spaceship would age more slowly than a person on Earth. Another surprising result is that mass can be changed into energy; this is the source of power in the atom bomb. The implications of relativity seem very mysterious to us, but it is only because we are not familiar with the conditions under which they are important. Most of these principles are important only for things moving at very high speeds, close to the speed of light.

Later, in 1915, Einstein produced a second part of his theory, the *general* theory of relativity. This deals with objects that are slowing down or speeding up, or are moving in curved paths. This theory gives a better understanding of space, gravity, and the nature of the universe.

ALSO READ: EINSTEIN, ALBERT.

RELIGION Religion is people's belief in some power greater than themselves. This power is often called *God*. God or gods have been known by various names throughout history. In Hinduism, the greatest God is called *Brahman*. In Judaism, the God's name is *Yahweh* or *Jehovah*. The Muslims call God *Allah*. Taoists believe in a supreme principle called *Tao*, meaning the "Way." Christians simply use the name *God*.

Basic Types of Religion Throughout human history, three basic types of religion have developed. The earli-

MAJOR RELIGIONS IN THE WORLD TODAY

Name	Founder	Where Founded	When Founded	Where Found Today	Number of Followers	Name of Followers
Buddhism	Gautama Buddha (about 563–483 B.C.)	India	About 500 B.C.	Cambodia, Laos, Vietnam, Thailand, Burma, China, Japan, Korea	311,836,000	Buddhists
Christianity	Jesus Christ (about 4 B.C.–A.D. 29)	Palestine (now Israel)	About A.D. 29	Mostly in Europe, Africa, North & South America, Australia	1,669,520,000	Christians
Confucianism	Confucius (551–478 B.C.)	China	400's B.C.	China	6,188,000	Confucians
Hinduism	(Founder unknown)	India	Between 3000 and 1500 B.C.	Mainly in India	663,495,000	Hindus
Islam	Muhammad (A.D. 570–632)	Arabia	A.D. 600's	Middle East, North Africa, Western Asia	880,552,000	Muslims
Judaism	Abraham (about 1700's B.C.)	Canaan (now Israel)	1700's B.C.	Mainly in U.S., Europe, Israel	18,169,000	Jews
Shintoism	(Founder unknown)	Japan	500's B.C.	Japan	3,379,000	Shintoists
Taoism	Lao-tse (about 604–531 B.C.)	China	500's B.C.	China	20,056,000	Taoists

est was *animism,* a belief that everything in nature has a spirit or soul of its own. Early people believed they were completely surrounded by these spirits—some of which were good, and some of which were evil. Human religion was aimed at encouraging the good spirits and protecting people from evil spirits. People held rain ceremonies, for example, so the rain spirit would water the crops. And they had ceremonies to make the evil spirits leave a sick person.

Polytheism is a belief in numerous gods. Each god ruled over certain areas of human life—war, love, agriculture, health, the home, and so on. The gods of polytheism were different from the spirits of animism. The gods were believed to have definite personalities, similar to those of human beings. They were not limited to living in natural objects, as the animistic spirits were. Thousand of tales were told about the great and wonderful deeds of these gods and goddesses. The mythologies of ancient Egypt,

Greece, Rome, the Norse countries, the Aztecs, and the Inca all contain legends about how the world was created, how mankind came to be, or how the world will end. People believed they could influence the gods and make agreements with them to ensure pleasant or successful outcomes to the events of life. Hinduism is the greatest polytheistic religion in the world today.

Monotheism is the belief in one all-powerful God. Judaism, Christianity, and Islam are the three great monotheistic religions of the modern world. A God of monotheism is believed to be aware of everything that happens in the world. The monotheistic God is believed to have created the world. This God is also believed to be the judge of human behavior, determining whether a person has lived a good life or not.

Most religions do not fit neatly into one or another of these types. Hinduism, for example, is polytheistic, but Hindus also believe in one supreme

▲ *Most priests of the Greek Orthodox Church have beards and wear black cassocks and hats. Their churches are richly decorated with religious art.*

▲ *Buddhist monks leave a temple after they have said their prayers.*

In the United States, 32 percent of the population is Protestant, and 22 percent is Roman Catholic. The Roman Catholic Church is, however, the largest single Christian body in the nation.

▶ *An archway in the Old City of Jerusalem frames the Dome of the Rock in the background. Jerusalem is a holy city for Christians, Jews, and Muslims.*

God, Brahman, who is greater than all the others. The teachings of Buddha do not even mention God, but Buddha stressed that people must treat each other with kindness in order to gain peace for themselves and for the world.

The various religions throughout the modern world are different not only in their gods but also in how believers worship them. Each religion usually has certain writings that are considered sacred—the *Bible* (Judaism—Old Testament; Christianity—Old and New Testament), the *Koran* (Islam), the *Bhagavad-Gita* (Hinduism), the *Tripitaka* (Buddhism), and the *Tao Te Ching* (Taoism). Each religion usually has one or more holy persons, or saints, who have inspired the faith of the people. In nearly every religion there are various *sects*, or branches. These are groups who believe in the basic faith of the religion but differ in how they follow or practice the religion. The Methodists, Presbyterians, Lutherans, Episcopalians, Greek Orthodox, and Catholics are some of the sects of Christianity. The Conservative, Reform, and Orthodox congregations are sects of Judaism.

Prayer and Sacrifice In all religions, believers feel themselves to

▲ *Muslims worship God at this mosque in Iraq in the Middle East. The mosque has a dome and graceful towers and is richly decorated with mosaics.*

have a relationship with their God or gods. What people do or don't do makes a difference in what will happen between them and their God. For this reason, almost all religions have some form of prayer. Prayer is people's way of speaking to their God. People use prayer to ask their God for help or protection. They also use prayer to praise their God and to thank the God for what has been done. In many religions, prayer is simply *meditation*—a way of getting to understand and know the God by silently thinking or contemplating about the God.

When people believe in a God, they sometimes feel they must give the God something. This is called *sacrifice*. People usually sacrifice to a God something that is very important to them. Early people used to sacrifice the first grains of their harvest or the first animals born in their flocks. This showed that they were willing to sacrifice something as important as their food in order to please the God.

Priesthood In the animistic spirit religions, the *shaman* (a medicine man or witch doctor) was believed to have magical powers. Shamans became very important because it was generally believed that they could speak directly to the spirits. Even tribal chiefs consulted a shaman before making important decisions.

As civilizations developed, people began to settle in towns and cities. A person often had his or her own house, and so it was felt that the gods should have their own houses, too. Temples, shrines, and holy places were set up. The people who dedicated themselves to serving the gods in the temples became known as priests. Priests led the prayers, offered the sacrifices, and made sure everyone contributed something to the god. The priests usually lived in the temples, and a high priest headed the religious organization of the community or kingdom.

In many countries, the priests became very powerful because the people believed that the priests' actions could influence the gods. The priests could also demand temple taxes, or *tithes*, with which to run the temples and at the same time make the gods happy. To keep the priesthood from gaining too much power, many kings made themselves head of the religion. They usually did this either by claiming to be a god or by claiming to be descended from a god. Thus the king had power over both the religion and the government. The pharaohs of ancient Egypt, the emperors of ancient China, and the Caesars of the Roman Empire are examples of rulers who were considered sacred and who were worshiped as gods.

The priests of modern-day religions are known by various names, such as minister, priest, rabbi, and imam. These religious leaders have charge of teaching their followers about their God and about their God's instructions for people. They conduct religious rituals and celebrations and help people in need.

Rites and Rituals The rites and rituals of a religion are the ways in which believers show their devotion to a god. There have been thousands of kinds of religious rituals throughout history. They differed according to the event being celebrated, the god being worshiped, and the traditions of the people doing the worshiping.

Most religious rituals center around the important events in life—birth, becoming an adult, marriage, death, harvest, planting time, and so on. All modern-day religions have, or once had, special rituals or ceremonies to celebrate these important occasions.

Many different objects have been used in the performance of rituals. Each object stands for, or symbolizes, a certain religious idea or belief. Food (bread and wine) is used in the services of many Christian sects and in the Jewish Passover meal. The Muslims use water to wash their feet before entering a mosque. Other religious rites have involved the use of incense, fire, special clothing, dances, music, and statues, and many other symbols.

Religious rites and rituals are usually very old. The Christian ritual of communion can be traced back to the Jewish Passover meal. The Passover meal itself has remained almost the same for the past 3,000 years and more. The rite of baptism is a very ancient one in many religions, marking the acceptance of the newborn child into the religious community.

The oldest known form of religious ritual was performed by the prehistoric Neanderthal people, who lived from 110,000 until 35,000 years ago. The Neanderthalers were the first people known to have buried their dead. They laid the bodies curled up in graves, and placed tools, food, and weapons with the bodies. These burials show that Neanderthal people were concerned about the mystery of death. What happens to a person when he or she dies? The Neanderthalers didn't know, but they wanted to be sure the dead had enough provisions to help them get along in their new kind of life. The Neanderthalers believed that people continue to live,

▲ *The Ganges River in India is considered holy by Hindus. Pilgrims gather at the water's edge to wash themselves and pray.*

The New Testament of the Bible was written in the days of the Roman Empire. It covers a period from the reign of King Herod to the fall of Jerusalem in A.D. 70. The first four books— Matthew, Mark, Luke, and John—were written soon after the death of Jesus, probably before A.D. 100. These books are called Gospels because the word means "good news"—the good news of Jesus' message for the world.

▲ *St. Ignatius of Loyola founded the Roman Catholic Society of Jesus in 1534. Its members, called Jesuits, have a special interest in education and missionary work.*

▲ A Girl with a Broom *by Rembrandt. Andrew Mellon Collection, National Gallery of Art, Washington, D.C.*

even though they die. This belief is a basic feature of almost all religions—that after death, human beings join another world, a world of the spirit, where they keep on living.

For further information on:

Religions of the World, *see* BUD-DHISM, CHRISTIANITY, CHRISTIAN SCIENCE, HINDUISM, ISLAM, JUDAISM, LATTER-DAY SAINTS, ORTHODOX CHURCH, PROTESTANT CHURCHES, PURITAN, ROMAN CATHOLIC CHURCH, SOCIETY OF FRIENDS, TAOISM, WITCHCRAFT.

Religious Holidays, *see* CHRISTMAS, EASTER, HANUKKAH, PASSOVER, YOM KIPPUR.

Religious Leaders, *see* AQUINAS, THOMAS; BECKET, THOMAS A; BUDDHA; CLERGY; CONFUCIUS; EDWARD THE CONFESSOR; EVANGELIST; FRANCIS OF ASSISI; JESUS CHRIST; JOAN OF ARC; LUTHER, MARTIN; MISSIONARY; MORE, SIR THOMAS; MUHAMMAD; NICHOLAS, SAINT; PROPHET; SAINT; SMITH, JOSEPH; WESLEY, JOHN AND CHARLES; YOUNG, BRIGHAM.

Religious Movements, *see* CHURCH AND STATE, CRUSADES, JEWISH HISTORY, PROTESTANT REFORMATION.

Religious Places, *see* CATACOMBS, CATHEDRAL, GANGES RIVER, JERUSALEM, MONASTERY, MOSQUE, PAGODA, PALESTINE, VATICAN CITY, WESTMINSTER ABBEY.

Religious Rites, *see* BURIAL CUSTOMS, MARRIAGE.

Religious Traditions and Writings, *see* BIBLE, DEAD SEA SCROLLS, GODS AND GODDESSES, KORAN, MYTHOLOGY.

REMBRANDT VAN RIJN (1606–1669) Even a short list of the world's greatest artists would include the name of the great Dutch master, Rembrandt van Rijn. The Netherlands of the 1600's produced many great painters, but Rembrandt outshines them all.

He was born in the town of Leiden, the sixth of seven children of a middle-class miller. He must have been an intelligent child because he was chosen to be sent to the local Latin school. Later, he entered the University of Leiden but left after a short time to become an artist's apprentice.

He moved between Leiden and Amsterdam, finally opening a studio at the age of 19 in Amsterdam. Rembrandt never studied in Italy, the world center of painting in his time. As far as we know, he never even went there to see the works of Michelangelo, Raphael, and other great artists. He studied with teachers who had been abroad. Rembrandt stayed within the borders of his country, working hard all his life, drawing, etching, and painting.

Look at his painting, *A Girl with a Broom*. See how a soft light picks her out of the surrounding gloom. This girl, lost in deep thought, leans on her well-used broom. What thoughts are going on behind those dream-filled eyes? The picture makes you wonder. Rembrandt could raise such a question with his portraits.

The girl's face is modeled by light. See the highlight on the forehead. Notice how her nose fades off into shadow on one side of her face. A special light brings out the red of her hair and the red bodice she is wearing. But all around her—becoming darker at the edge of the canvas—is gloom. This was Rembrandt's way of painting. He was a master of light and shadow—*chiaroscuro*, artists call it.

Rembrandt did many portraits during his lifetime. He painted people of all ages and many occupations. At the times in life when he was poor, he painted members of his family or the servants. The girl in this painting was probably a servant girl. She appears in several of his works done around the year 1650. Rembrandt did many self-portraits, from the time he was a young painter until he was a very old man. He had a collection of unusual headdresses and costumes that he would sometimes wear to change his looks when he used himself for a model.

Rembrandt's etchings and drawings were more famous than his paintings during his lifetime. Many of his pictures in all techniques showed scenes from the Bible. In the centuries since he lived, people have come to see the greatness of his paintings. They are among the most prized possessions of art museums.

■ LEARN BY DOING

Can you see how Rembrandt has used triangles in his composition? See how the arms, the hands, and the head form one triangle. Then, an opposing triangle comes from the angle of the broom, three flashes of red bodice, and the angle of the overturned bucket.

Try drawing a simple portrait of a friend or one of your family, using triangles in the composition. You will learn some of the problems a portrait painter faces. ■

ALSO READ: DUTCH AND FLEMISH ART.

RENAISSANCE The word Renaissance means "rebirth." Even in the 1400's, in Italy, when this great search for knowledge and awakening of interest in the arts was taking place, people referred to the time as such. People were rediscovering the glories of ancient Greece and Rome, and they considered this exciting time a rebirth.

The Renaissance brought a new spirit of learning to Europe. Printing with movable type was invented in Europe, along with new ways of making paper. America was discovered, and Magellan proved the world was round by sailing around it. A great struggle for religious reform came in the Protestant Reformation. Copernicus and Galileo made discoveries that established astronomy as a new sci-

ence. Great discoveries were also taking place in art and architecture. Why so many great artists lived at this time is impossible to explain. It was a time of genius when Western art changed, grew, and flourished.

Renaissance art began in the early 1400's in the Italian city of Florence. Some artists and architects set out to create new art. One of the leaders was an architect, Filippo Brunelleschi. It is said that he measured the ruins of old Roman palaces and temples. He did not copy the old buildings but combined the ancient plans with his own to come up with a new kind of architecture. His architectural ideas were still being used 500 years later. The Pazzi Chapel in Florence is one very famous church that he designed.

Brunelleschi also discovered *perspective*—how to give a three-dimensional look on the flat surface of a painting. Artists began using perspective almost at once. With perspective, they could make objects in a painting look close up or far away. The Florentine artist, Masaccio, was one of the first artists to use perspective.

Donatello, a great sculptor in Florence during the early Renaissance, had new ideas about sculpture. In his statue of David, the slayer of Goliath (shown here), he tried to capture the appearance of a teenage boy. Donatello carefully studied the human form before doing this sculpture.

About the same time as Donatello, another sculptor, Claus Sluter, was working in the court of the Duke of Burgundy (in what is now France). Sluter also created sculpture that accurately showed the human form. In the country of Flanders (now in Belgium), a painter named Jan van Eyck was experimenting with oil painting. Painters before van Eyck had used egg tempera—powdered paints mixed with egg. Van Eyck was probably the first to use oil. He had found that egg tempera dried too quickly. He began using oil so that his paint

▲ *Rembrandt painted this self-portrait around 1660.*

▲ David *by Donatello.*

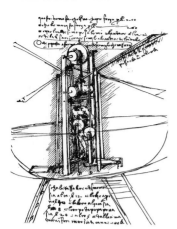

▲ *A sketch for a flying machine by Leonardo da Vinci.*

▼ *St. Peter's, Rome, as seen from the Vatican Gardens. The buildings shown here were designed by Michelangelo. They include the famous dome that he helped to design. It was built in the 1500's.*

work more slowly and pay attention to detail.

One of van Eyck's masterpieces is the picture shown with the article on MARRIAGE, *Giovanni Arnolfini and His Bride.* The young man and his bride touch hands tenderly as they pose in their new home. The picture was painted in 1434, and in it you can see many details of a home of that time—the chandelier hanging over the young couple, the slippers left carelessly on the floor, even the little family dog! Van Eyck opened a new world of detail that painters continued to show for hundreds of years.

During the 1400's, artists in Italy, Flanders, and elsewhere began to experiment with new methods and styles of painting. The city of Florence took tremendous pride in its artists, and many masters were trained in its workshops. Leonardo da Vinci studied there, in the workshop of Andrea del Verrocchio, a well-known painter and sculptor. Leonardo became more than a master painter. He was a genius who developed amazingly accurate theories in biology, engineering, physics, chemistry, architecture, war, how the human body works, and many other subjects. His notebooks and sketches

▲ *Madonna and Child and Angels by Botticelli shows the warm, gentle beauty of his paintings.*

have been saved. They contain thousands of ideas, questions, and theories that he kept in secret journals. The illustration shows his sketch for a flying machine—a few hundred years ahead of his time.

Michelangelo Buonarroti, born 23 years after Leonardo, was apprenticed to the Florentine painter, Domenico Ghirlandaio. While learning from his master, he worked at developing his own style. Michelangelo wanted to know all about the human body in order to draw, paint, and sculpt it accurately. Michelangelo was asked by Pope Julian II to paint frescoes for the walls and ceiling of the Sistine Chapel. He spent four years creating this masterpiece, all the time protesting that he was a sculptor, not a painter.

In 1504, a young painter, Raphael (Raffaello Sanzio in Italian), arrived in Florence. He studied the work of Leonardo and Michelangelo. In a few years, he also went to Rome, where Pope Julian II asked him to paint frescoes for some rooms of the Vatican. Raphael had learned well the techniques of Leonardo and Michelangelo and used them to produce his own style. His Madonnas have become particularly famous.

Several other master painters were working at this time. Titian, Giorgione, Tintoretto, Veronese, and Correggio were among the great painters of the city of Venice. Other artists were Fra Bartolommeo, Fra Filippo Lippi, Fra Angelico, Piero della Francesca, Mantegna, and Botticelli.

The influence of Italian Renaissance art spread to other countries. Artists from all over Europe went to Florence, Venice, and other Italian cities to study. France, following the lead of Italy, began training and supporting its own artists late in the 1400's. In the 1600's the Renaissance came to Spain. In architecture, this brought the building of great cathedrals in that country. Somewhat later, the artists El Greco and Diego Velázquez painted their magnificent works. The Renaissance moved north to Germany and to the Low Countries, where the Flemish and Dutch artists flourished. Renaissance ideas at last moved across the channel to England, where the Renaissance style in architecture influenced Christopher Wren in his design of St. Paul's Cathedral in London. By 1650, the Renaissance thirst for knowledge and for new ideas and techniques in art and architecture had finally spread throughout Europe.

ALSO READ: ARCHITECTURE, ART HISTORY, BAROQUE PERIOD, EL GRECO, GIOTTO, ITALIAN HISTORY, LEONARDO DA VINCI, MICHELANGELO BUONARROTI, MIDDLE AGES, RAPHAEL, REMBRANDT VAN RIJN, SCULPTURE, TITIAN.

RENOIR, PIERRE AUGUSTE
(1841–1919) Pierre Auguste Renoir was one of the leaders of the Impressionists. His paintings were laughed at and rejected for many years. But people came to appreciate the gently

rounded forms and the soft, warm colors of the ideal world he painted, and his works became very popular.

Renoir was born in Limoges, France. He grew up in Paris. Renoir liked to call himself a "workman-painter" rather than an artist, because he came from a family of craftworkers. He was proud to be descended from a shoemaker, a tailor, and a carpenter. He himself became an apprentice porcelain painter at 14, painting designs on fine china. The money he earned at this trade paid for lessons in drawing at the Academy of Fine Arts when he was 21. Several long, hard years of study and work followed. Then Renoir and his friend, Claude Monet, began working together perfecting the newly discovered way of painting outdoors, with separate touches of vivid color. In 1874, painters using this technique were named "Impressionists." Renoir's painting soon began to attract attention. The outstanding work of this period is *Dancing at the Moulin de la Galette* (seen on page 2086).

■ LEARN BY DOING
Renoir painted this large canvas entirely out-of-doors. See the dappled light effects of sun and shadow he

▲ *Michelangelo's marble masterpiece, the* Pietà, *depicts Mary holding the dead Jesus just taken down from the cross. The statue was damaged in 1972 at the Vatican.*

▲ *Angelo Dori, a rich gentleman, is remembered today because the great artist Raphael painted his portrait.*

▲ Dancing at the Moulin de la Galette *by Pierre Auguste Renoir.*

uses? Study the picture a while, and you will see how he shows the happy feeling of these young people at an outdoor dance hall. Some of Renoir's friends are sitting at the table at the right. Each day they would help him carry the huge canvas outside at the dance hall, so he could work on it. How do Renoir's colors help give a pleasant, friendly feeling to this scene? ■

When Renoir was 40, he married a 19-year-old girl, Aline Charigot. She was the model for the portrait shown here, and for many of Renoir's paintings. He settled down into a happy

▼ Girl with a Straw Hat *by Pierre Auguste Renoir.*

family life. He continued to experiment with and expand his painting techniques. He kept on painting for the rest of his life. On the day he died, he remarked as he put away his brushes after painting, "I think I am beginning to understand something about it."

ALSO READ: ART, IMPRESSIONISM.

REPORTER see JOURNALISM, NEWSPAPER.

REPRODUCTION Reproduction is the way an organism (a living thing—plant or animal) gives rise to another organism like itself. All organisms must reproduce in order to survive. This is done in several different ways.

Reproduction can be *asexual* or *sexual*. In asexual reproduction, there is only one parent. In sexual reproduction, there are two parents.

Asexual Reproduction Many simple plants and animals reproduce asexually. The simplest kind of asexual reproduction is *fission*, or division. The organism splits in half, and each half becomes, or is, a separate organism.

Budding is another kind of asexual reproduction. The parent organism grows a bump, called a *bud*. The bud gets bigger and stronger until it is a complete organism able to live by itself. Then it drops off the parent and starts a life of its own. Sometimes the buds do not drop off. They remain together in a collection of organisms called a *colony*. Certain sponges are colonies of organisms formed by budding.

Bacteria, protozoa, and all plants except seed plants reproduce by forming *spores*. Each spore contains a few cells from the parent. The cells are usually wrapped in a hard, protective coating. A spore may be carried

▲ *A bee aids in the sexual reproduction of a flower. Pollen sticks to its body and is carried from one blossom to another.*

BLACKBERRY STOLON

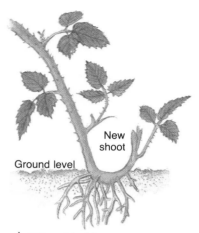

▲ *When blackberry stems arch over and touch the ground, a new plant develops. The stems are called* stolons.

far away by wind or water. If it is dropped in a suitable place, it will begin to divide and develop into a new organism.

Vegetative reproduction is common in plants. Part of the plant sends out roots and grows shoots. Eventually this part produces a complete new plant. The part may become separated from the parent plant or it may remain attached to it. Examples of these parts are *bulbs*, *corms*, *tubers*, and *rhizomes*. Vegetative reproduction also occurs in simple animals, for example by budding.

Sexual Reproduction In sexual reproduction, a male sex cell, called a *sperm*, joins with, or *fertilizes*, a female cell, called an *ovum* or egg, to form one fertilized cell. This fertilized cell divides over and over until a whole new organism has been formed.

The sex cells are produced by sex organs in the bodies of the parent organisms. In most animals, the sexes are separated—the male animals produce the male sex cells, the female animals produce the female cells. In some animals and in most plants, each organism has both male and female sex organs and, therefore, produces both kind of sex cells. But even then the male and female cells from the same organism do not usually join together. A male cell from one organism fertilizes the female cell of another.

Unlike asexual reproduction, the type that results in offspring identical to the single parent, sexual reproduction produces offspring that share some features of both parents. This is because the mother provides half the information about what the offspring is going to look like, and the father provides the other half. The information is carried by the chromosomes, tiny threads in the *nucleus* (core) of the sex cells.

Every mature sex cell contains only half as many chromosomes as every body cell. A human body cell contains 23 *pairs* of matched chromosomes, while a human sex cell, male or female, only contains 23 single chromosomes (one of each pair). You might say that a body cell answers every question twice. The body cell has two chromosomes with two genes (bits of information) determining what the eye color is going to be. A sex cell carries only one chromosome with a gene for eye color, so it has only one gene for eye color.

The way in which pairs of chromosomes, as in the body cells, divide to become single chromosomes, as in the sex cells, is called *meiosis*. In meiosis, the pairs of chromosomes line up opposite each other in the nucleus. Then they separate, one chromosome from each pair going to each end of the nucleus. Then the nucleus divides in half, forming two nuclei. Each nucleus has one member of each chromosome pair. These nuclei divide again, so that four sex nuclei are eventually formed.

When a male sex cell joins with the female sex cell, the chromosomes are brought together in pairs again. One member of each pair comes from each parent. The new cell formed is called a *zygote*.

The zygote, or fertilized egg, divides into two cells. These two cells each divide to form four cells. The four divide into eight, and so forth.

▲ *Human male sperm cells as they appear under a high power electron microscope. Sperm are one of the smallest cells in the body. Their tails swing from side to side to push them along to the female egg.*

HOW LONG SOME ANIMALS TAKE TO DEVELOP

Human being 9 months
Elephant 20–22 months
Honeybee 3 days (from egg to larva)
Salmon 19–80 days depending on the temperature of the water in which the eggs are laid
Giant salamander 8–12 weeks
Hawk 3–4 weeks
Python about 2 weeks depending on the temperature when the eggs are laid
Dog 8–9 weeks
Cat 9 weeks
Rat 3 weeks
Kangaroo 6 weeks

Each of these cells contains the same chromosomes as the zygote. This kind of division, in which both members of each pair of chromosomes are passed on, is *mitosis*.

The divisions happen very quickly, and soon the embryo is a tight ball of cells. Then the cells begin to *differentiate*. If it is an animal embryo, some cells form an outer skin for the embryo; other cells begin to form a stomach; still others form blood and muscle. The study of the development of embryos is called *embryology*.

FERTILIZATION AND DEVELOPMENT. Fertilization for sexual reproduction takes place in different ways. In flowering plants, both the male sex cells, or sperm, and female sex cells, or ova (eggs), are produced in the flower. The pollen containing the sperm is formed in the stamens. The pollen from one flower is carried to the pistil of another flower by insects, wind, or water. The sperm from the pollen enter the long stalk of the pistil and fertilize the eggs. The eggs are produced by the ovary at the base of the flower. Fertilization results in a seed, a part of which is an embryo. Often the *ovary* swells up to form a protective fruit. These fruits, with seeds inside, are eaten by birds or other animals. The fruit is digested, but the undigestible seeds pass unharmed through the animal and are expelled. If a seed falls on soil where it can grow, it will send out roots and stems and develop into a new plant.

Many other plants fertilize and reproduce in similar ways. The parts that are found in the flowers of flowering plants are found elsewhere in plants that do not have flowers. Some plants alternate sexual and asexual reproduction. One generation reproduces sexually, the next generation reproduces asexually, and then the next sexually again. Ferns and mosses alternate like this.

In animals, fertilization may be *internal* or *external*. Internal fertilization takes place inside the body of the female. External fertilization takes place outside the body.

In external fertilization, the female lays the eggs and the male fertilizes them after she has laid them. In order for the sperm to penetrate the egg, the egg cannot have a hard shell. An egg without a shell would dry out on land, so external fertilization usually takes place in water. Fishes and amphibians (frogs and salamanders) reproduce this way.

In most land animals and birds, fertilization is internal. The male inserts the sperm directly into the female's body, where the sperm unites with the egg to form the embryo. The embryo may then develop externally or internally. In external development, the embryo, together with some food (egg yolk), is covered with a hard shell and is laid as an egg. In internal development, the embryo de-

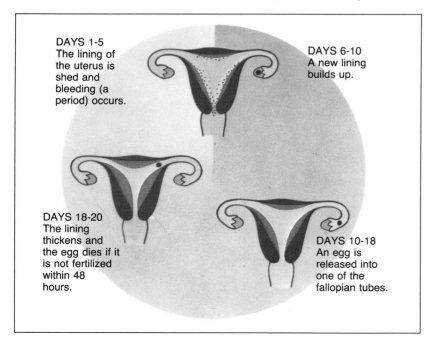

DAYS 1-5
The lining of the uterus is shed and bleeding (a period) occurs.

DAYS 6-10
A new lining builds up.

DAYS 18-20
The lining thickens and the egg dies if it is not fertilized within 48 hours.

DAYS 10-18
An egg is released into one of the fallopian tubes.

◄ *The main stages in the human female menstrual (monthly) cycle. At the start of the cycle the lining of the* uterus (womb) *is shed, which causes bleeding. A new lining then builds up in preparation for an egg to be released from the ovary into one of the fallopian tubes during* ovulation. *If the egg is not fertilized, the egg and lining are shed and a new cycle begins.*

▲ *A ewe suckles her newborn lamb. Newborn lambs, foals, and other herd animals struggle to their feet almost as soon as they are born.*

velops in a womb inside the mother's body.

The number of offspring a mother gives birth to at one time depends on the number of eggs fertilized. In human mothers, only one egg is usually fertilized. If more than one is fertilized, the mother may have a *multiple birth*—twins, triplets, or even more. *Identical twins* are produced when a single fertilized egg divides into two separate cells; these daughter cells contain exactly the same chromosomes and go on to develop into two offspring that are alike in every way.

Animals that take care of their young for a long time after birth usually only have a few offspring at a time. These offspring are often almost helpless at birth. Animals such as the green sea turtle, which don't care for their young after birth, often lay hundreds of eggs. They have to produce so many because only a few survive.

Other Kinds of Reproduction
Sometimes organisms reproduce in ways that cannot easily be called sexual or asexual. One-celled animals such as paramecia may reproduce by *conjugation*. Two animals simply join together and trade nuclear matter (matter from the inner core of their cells). Then they separate and each

▶ *Stages in the growth of a fetus, from the first division of cells to the perfectly-formed miniature human being eight weeks after fertilization.*

one divides twice to produce four new animals.

Some organisms, such as certain flatworms and jellyfish, can reproduce sexually or asexually. In *parthenogenesis*, an egg that has not been fertilized develops into an embryo and then into a new organism. Bees reproduce this way. An unfertilized egg laid by the queen bee develops into a male drone; a fertilized egg becomes a female worker. A fertilized egg that is fed special food becomes a queen.

For further information on:
Alternation of Generations, *see* FERN, MOSSES AND LIVERWORTS.
Asexual Reproduction, *see* BACTERIA, MUSHROOM, PLANT BREEDING, PROTOZOAN, YEAST.
Genes and Chromosomes, *see* CELL, EVOLUTION, GENETICS.
Sexual Reproduction, *see* AMPHIBIAN, ANIMAL FAMILY, AUSTRALIAN MAMMALS, EGG, MAMMAL, MARSUPIAL, METAMORPHOSIS, PLANT, SEEDS AND FRUIT.

REPTILE A snake is a reptile—a cold-blooded, air-breathing animal with a backbone in its back and scales on its skin. Lizards are also reptiles. Snakes and lizards are close relatives and belong to the same *order* (group) of reptiles. The turtles are in another reptile order, and the alligators and crocodiles are members of a third order. The fourth, and last, order of reptiles has only one member—the tuatara, a strange little lizardlike animal that lives on a few islands off New Zealand.

The tuatara has not changed much in 200 million years. It is the closest surviving descendant of the first reptiles, the *cotylosaurs*. Cotylosaurs are

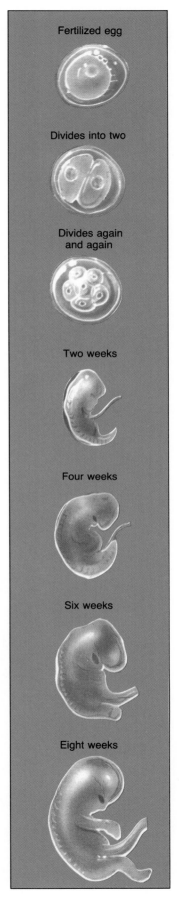

Fertilized egg

Divides into two

Divides again and again

Two weeks

Four weeks

Six weeks

Eight weeks

▲ *Turtles are reptiles that have roamed the earth since the days of the dinosaurs. They survived basically because their shells protect them from enemies. The box turtle can withdraw totally into its shell.*

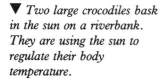

▼ *Two large crocodiles bask in the sun on a riverbank. They are using the sun to regulate their body temperature.*

called stem reptiles because all of the other reptiles stemmed—branched out—from them. Among the branches were the turtles, the crocodiles, the lizards, the *therapsids*—the reptiles that gave rise to mammals—and the dinosaurs.

The time when the dinosaurs lived is called the age of the reptiles. It fell midway between the age of the amphibians and the age of mammals, just as reptiles fall midway in development between amphibians on the one hand and mammals and birds on the other. Amphibians gave rise to reptiles. Reptiles gave rise to mammals and birds.

Reptiles inherited the egg from the amphibians. But the reptiles greatly improved the amphibian egg. They made it watertight, not to keep water out but to keep juices in. Amphibians had to lay their eggs in water to keep them from drying out. Reptiles could lay their eggs on land. This allowed them to become the first true land animals. Some reptiles have gone even further and give birth to live young. This characteristic was passed on to the mammals, while egg-laying was passed on to the birds.

Reptiles are often said to be "cold-blooded," like the amphibians, as opposed to the "warm-blooded" birds and mammals. This does not mean that their blood is always cold. It just

means that their temperature changes with the temperature of their surroundings. If a reptile lives in a warm place and stays active, its temperature may be higher than that of many warm-blooded animals.

Reptile Orders The turtle developed in the age of the dinosaurs and has not changed very much since then. It has not changed because armor has enabled it to survive without changing. Every turtle has some sort of shell. In some turtles, this shell is only a thick, leathery skin, but in most turtles, it is a double layer of hard, horny scales and tightly fitted bones.

The shell is wonderful for protection, but it is not so good for other things. In order to walk, every turtle has to slide its shoulders back into its rib cage. In order to breathe, it has to rearrange its insides. Getting the head into the shell is a problem. Most turtles curl their necks up into an S-shape.

The crocodilians—including crocodiles and alligators—are almost as old as the turtle. And although they are very old, crocodiles and alligators are very modern in some ways. They are the only reptiles with four-chambered hearts, like a human heart. Crocodiles and alligators may live to be over 50 years old and grow up to 20 feet (6 m)

long. Like most reptiles, they eat meat. Occasionally a crocodile or an alligator may attack a human being, but such attacks are rare.

Lizards and snakes are the most successful reptiles. Of the approximately 5,000 different species (kinds) of reptiles, about 3,000 are lizards and about 2,700 are snakes. A couple of snakes have tiny vestigial (leftover, almost useless) legs, and a few lizards are legless. But all lizards have eyelids, and no snakes have eyelids—a snake's eyes are always open. The scales on a lizard's skin are about the same all over, while a snake usually has a special row of wide, flat scales on its belly. The snake can grip the ground with these scales to move itself about. Lizards have outside ears, and snakes do not. Most lizards can drop off their tails for protection and grow new ones. Snakes cannot.

For further information on:
Individual Reptiles, *see* ALLIGATORS AND CROCODILES, LIZARD, SNAKE, TURTLE.
Reptile Characteristics, *see* ANIMAL DEFENSES, ANIMAL MOVEMENT, EGG, MOLTING, REGENERATION, REPRODUCTION, RESPIRATION, VERTEBRATE.

▼ *A cornered grass snake plays dead. But its posture and open, relaxed jaws are only to fool its enemies.*

Reptile Evolution, *see* AMPHIBIAN, BIRDS OF THE PAST, DINOSAUR, EVOLUTION, FOSSIL, MAMMAL, RARE ANIMAL.

REPUBLIC A nation that does not have a king, or queen, or some other monarch as leader of the government is called a republic. A monarch inherits his or her position as head of the government, but the leader of a republic comes to power through other means.

Most modern republics have come into being as the result of revolution and overthrow of a monarch. The 13 colonies of North America were ruled by the British monarch until 1776. During the American Revolution, the colonies overthrew British monarchical rule and established a republican form of government in which its President and lawmakers (senators and representatives) were elected by the people. In 1789, the French people overthrew their monarch and set up a republic. Even though Napoleon destroyed the French republic in 1804, the idea of an elected government became very popular throughout Europe. By the 1940's, the United Kingdom and the Dutch and Scandinavian monarchies were the only non-republican governments in Europe.

The word "republic" is often confused with "democracy." A republic can be a democracy when the people directly elect the officials of the government, and when these elected officials follow the will of the people. But a republic can also be a dictatorship in which top officials are not elected by the people directly, or in which the officials do not follow the will of the people.

The earliest republics known in detail are the city-states of ancient Greece. Except for slaves, each citizen of a Greek city had a vote in choosing government leaders, and any citizen could be elected to office. The ancient Romans also formed a republic that lasted until 27 B.C., after which Rome

▲ *A frilled lizard puts on its threatening display.*

There are over 5,000 living species of reptiles. The largest is the estuarine crocodile, which can be as long as 25 feet (7.6 m) and weigh well over 1,000 pounds (450 kg).

▲ *The ancient Roman republic lasted until 27* B.C. *Under the republic, the* forum, *shown above, served as a marketplace, a law court, and as a setting for parades, political meetings, and spectacles.*

In ancient times, people thought that a person's breath was actually the life spirit. The word "inspiration" comes from two Latin words meaning "to breathe into." So when you are inspired, something has put breath—or spirit and life—into you.

A person at rest breathes in and out some 13 times a minute. With each breath, about 30 cubic inches (500 cc) of air is taken in.

became a monarchy run by emperors. The word "republic" comes from the Latin term *res publica*, meaning "public affair." The oldest existing republic is probably the tiny country of San Marino (located in Italy, north of Rome). It was founded as a republic in the A.D. 300's. Switzerland organized as a republic in 1291. With few exceptions, most countries today have republican governments.

ALSO READ: AMERICAN REVOLUTION; DEMOCRACY; GOVERNMENT; GREECE, ANCIENT; NATION; REVOLUTION; ROME, ANCIENT.

RESERVOIR see WATER SUPPLY.

RESIN see SYNTHETIC.

RESONANCE see SOUND.

▶ *Oxygen that has just been inhaled passes into the bloodstream in tiny parts of the lungs called* alveoli. *Each alveolus has a wall only one cell thick. Oxygen passes into the blood vessels and combines with the red blood cells to be carried around the body. The waste carbon dioxide from all parts of the body moves from the blood into the alveolus.*

RESPIRATION All living things must have energy. They obtain this energy through respiration, a process that changes food to energy. Most living things use *oxygen* in respiration. Oxygen is an element (basic chemical substance) that combines very readily with other elements in a process called oxidation. Burning is a kind of oxidation, and rusting is another kind. In oxidation, new chemical compounds (combinations) are formed and energy is produced.

Most living things get their oxygen from the air or from the water. The oxygen passes to the cells where it is used to oxidize (burn) food. Oxidation produces energy, carbon dioxide, and water. The energy is used for the work and growth of the cell. The carbon dioxide and water are given off as waste.

Plants and simple animals have no trouble obtaining oxygen. Their cells absorb (soak up) oxygen directly from the air or water they live in. But in larger animals only a few cells are in direct contact with air or water. Most of their cells are buried deep within their bodies, and oxygen must reach them through a respiratory system.

The respiratory systems of many animals are composed of *respiratory organs* that pick up oxygen from their

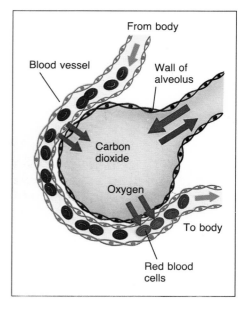

surroundings. These respiratory organs have thin, wet walls and a good supply of blood. The *gills* of a fish pick up oxygen from water. The *lungs* of human beings and other land animals pick up oxygen from the air. The oxygen then passes through the thin walls of the respiratory organ into the blood, where it combines (joins) with the red blood cells. The blood carries the oxygen through smaller and smaller blood vessels until it reaches the thin-walled vessels called *capillaries*. The oxygen passes through the walls of the capillaries and into the cells, where oxidation takes place. The waste carbon dioxide and water given off by oxidation go back into the blood and are carried to the respiratory organ.

In the respiratory organ, the blood cells give off the carbon dioxide and water and pick up fresh oxygen. The carbon dioxide and water leave the body. When you breathe in, you bring oxygen in the air into your body. When you breathe out, you are forcing out carbon dioxide and water, in the form of vapor.

The blood of insects does not carry oxygen. Oxygen enters the body through small openings, called *spiracles*, and passes into tubes called *tracheae*. The tracheae carry the oxygen to all parts of the body.

ALSO READ: ARTIFICIAL RESPIRATION, BLOOD, BREATHING, DIGESTION, NOSE.

RESTAURANT Restaurants prepare and sell food and drink. There are many types of restaurants, including cafeterias, soda fountains (in drugstores and dime stores), coffeehouses, tearooms, roadside and drive-in restaurants, and restaurants that specialize in the food of one particular country. Some restaurants offer a *menu* (list of foods served) of hotdogs and hamburgers at an average cost of less than two dollars. Others offer a variety of full meals prepared to de-

light the most particular diner—at a much higher price.

The type of service that customers get depends on the kind of restaurant they are in. Customers in cafeterias (similar to the one that may be in your school) see the available food and choose what they please. They may serve themselves (buffet-style) or be served by waiters. In many restaurants, customers are seated first, and the food they select from the menu is brought to them.

A restaurant owner must have a large staff to run the business efficiently. The headwaiter or host seats customers and sometimes takes their orders. Waiters serve the food, and assistants set and clear the tables. The chef (head cook) and other cooks prepare the meals. (The chef sometimes plans the menu as well.) Dishwashers and janitors are necessary, too.

Eating out has not always been as popular as it is today. Before the 1800's, people almost always had their meals at home. They ate at inns, taverns, and other restaurants only when they were traveling. Many taverns and coffeehouses were also popular meeting places—for writers, politicians, and ordinary people who just wanted an evening out.

Early restaurants served only one kind of meal, at one price, at a certain time. The meal was known by the French words *table d'hôte*, meaning "table of the host." This expression is still used to mean a full meal (appetizer, main course, and dessert) served at a fixed price. French restaurants added the custom of serving meals *a la carte*, meaning "by the menu." Customers were given a list of the foods that were available, and they could make their choice. The first American restaurant (that was separate from a hotel) was Delmonico's, which opened in 1827 in New York City.

As towns and cities grew, so did the need for more restaurants. Many people could no longer get home easily

▲ *An outdoor cafe in Vienna, Austria. Such restaurants are popular in Europe, especially in countries around the Mediterranean.*

It is impossible to state which was the first restaurant in the world, but one of the earliest bearing that name was opened in Madrid, Spain in the 1720's. One of its dishwashers was the famous Spanish painter Goya!

The highest restaurants in the world are those to be found at the top of ski lift stations on mountain ski resorts.

▲ *Restaurants are meeting places where people come to enjoy good food and the company of their friends.*

Later in life, Paul Revere was successful in various business enterprises, including shipping ice to the West Indies.

▲ *An engraving of Paul Revere's ride to Concord to warn the people of the approach of British troops.*

for lunch. In the late 1800's, a new kind of self-service restaurant—the cafeteria—was opened. At first, there were separate cafeterias for men and women. In this century, cafeterias and other fast-food restaurants have become very popular. As more and more people traveled by automobile, roadside restaurants, carry-out restaurants, and drive-ins were opened to meet their needs.

REVERE, PAUL (1735–1818)

Listen, my children, and you
    shall hear
Of the midnight ride of Paul
    Revere . . .

You may have heard these famous lines of poetry by Henry Wadsworth Longfellow about one of the heroes of the American Revolution. Paul Revere was a Boston silversmith and patriot. He is remembered for his brave ride through the Massachusetts countryside to warn the farmers that British troops were coming.

Revere was born in Boston, Massachusetts. He was the third of 12 children of a silversmith. Paul learned the trade from his father and became a master craftsman. Many of the fine silver pieces he designed still survive. Revere also cast bells and made cannon in his foundry. He produced bolts, spikes, pumps, and copper parts for the ship *Old Ironsides*. He

designed the first issue of Continental money and the seal of the state of Massachusetts, which the state still uses.

Revere was an active patriot. He donned war paint and feathers to take part in the Boston Tea Party. He often served as a messenger for revolutionary colonial organizations. On the night of April 18, 1775, Revere learned that the British planned to attack Lexington and Concord. He arranged a signal to warn of the British "secret" move. If they moved by land, one lantern would be hung in the steeple of Boston's Old North Church. If by sea, two lanterns would be hung.

When Revere learned that the British were coming by sea, he gave the signal. Then he rode toward Concord with William Dawes and Samuel Prescott. The three were stopped by a British patrol. Revere was captured and Dawes escaped. Only Prescott rode on to warn Concord. Revere was released later that night. He is believed to have been in Lexington just in time to hear the first shots of the revolution fired.

ALSO READ: AMERICAN REVOLUTION; BOSTON TEA PARTY; LONGFELLOW, HENRY WADSWORTH.

REVOLUTION A revolution is a method of overthrowing an old system of government and establishing a new one, giving power to those who have overthrown the old order. Revolutions have occurred throughout history for many reasons. A revolution is usually begun when many people in a country become unhappy with the way the country is being run. The government may be too strict with its citizens. It may tax them too heavily. Its laws may be unfair to many. A strong person, or group of persons, may lead other dissatisfied people toward revolution. When the people think they have enough power, they try to take over the government. Some revolutions have been long and bloody, lasting many years. Others have involved little bloodshed. Sometimes, after a revolution has been successful, another group rises up against it. This movement is called a *counterrevolution.*

The American Revolution began because many of the British colonies in North America wanted to separate from England. They resented being governed from abroad and paying unfair taxes. In 1775, they went to war with England. After six years of fighting, the colonies won their independence, and the United States was born. The French Revolution was brought about by the royal family's unjust rule. Most of the people lived in poverty. The people arose against the monarchy and the wealthy ruling class. The king, queen, and many of the nobility were beheaded. In October 1911, the Chinese Revolution began. It was led by Sun Yat-sen against the ruling Manchu dynasty (line of royalty). China then became a republic. The Russian Revolution in 1917

ended the reign of the czars (kings) and led to the establishment of a Communist government. Russia became the Union of Soviet Socialist Republics. Soviet troops put down the Hungarian Revolution of 1956. The Cuban Revolution of 1959 brought Fidel Castro to power, and Iran's revolution in 1979 ended the shah's rule. In February 1986, the government of the Philippines under President Marcos was overthrown in a generally nonviolent rebellion, ending a dictatorship of some 20 years.

A *coup d'état* is a kind of revolution in which one group, usually the military, overthrows the constitutional government. Some countries in Latin America and Africa have frequent coups d'état or rebellions.

ALSO READ: AMERICAN REVOLUTION; CASTRO, FIDEL; FRENCH REVOLUTION; IRAN; RUSSIAN HISTORY; SUN YAT-SEN.

▲ *Vladimir Illyich Lenin, the Bolshevik leader who headed the new Soviet Union after the Russian Revolution of 1917.*

▼ *The riots outside St. Stephen's Cathedral in Vienna, Austria, were just part of the general social, economic, and political unrest in Europe that came to be known as the Revolutions of 1848.*

REYNOLDS, JOSHUA (1723–1792) Reynolds was the first of several great English portrait painters. He was born in Plympton, Devonshire. When he was 26, he traveled to Italy, where he studied for two years and saw the works of the great Italian masters.

He returned to London and became a portrait painter, which was the only kind of painter in great demand in England at that time. He painted portraits of many British political and artistic leaders. Reynolds tried to get to know the people whose portraits he painted. He did not just copy faces and costumes. In some way, he wanted to bring out each sitter's personality.

What can you tell about the personality of little George Hare in the portrait shown here? Little boys wore dresses in those days, and George's has fallen down over one shoulder. Reynolds may be saying that George is an active boy who would rather be playing than sitting for his portrait.

▲ George Hare, *a portrait by Joshua Reynolds.*

▲ Lord Heathfield (detail), a portrait by Joshua Reynolds. It was painted to commemorate Lord Heathfield's defense of Gibraltar during a long siege and conveys the strength and character of its subject.

▼ Barges travel down the Rhine River in West Germany past lovely towns and castles, green fields, and vineyards.

Why do you suppose George is pointing off into the distance? The pointing finger tends to make your eye follow it out of the picture. Reynolds cleverly balanced that arm with the fallen down sleeve on the opposite side of the picture. The horizontal sash also helps pull your eye back into the picture.

Reynolds was a master of composition. He often experimented with new kinds of paint, and many of his paintings have deteriorated over the years. He was also a famous teacher of the principles of art.

RHINE RIVER   The Rhine is one of the major rivers of Europe. It begins in the Alps Mountains of Switzerland. The river then flows northward for about 820 miles (1,320 km) through Switzerland, Liechtenstein, Austria, West Germany, France, and the Netherlands. At Rotterdam in the Netherlands, the Rhine empties into the North Sea. (See the map with the article on EUROPE.)

The Rhine River is an important transportation route in Europe. It is navigable by oceangoing ships as far as Mannheim, West Germany, and by river barges as far as Basel, Switzerland. Raw materials, such as oil, are transported up the Rhine River to industrial areas, such as the Ruhr in West Germany. Many Swiss and German manufactured goods are carried down the Rhine for export abroad.

South of the West German capital of Bonn, the Rhine flows through a rugged valley. Grapes grown on the steep hillsides produce the famous Rhine wines. This area is the legendary home of the *Lorelei*, a beautiful Rhine maiden whose singing lured sailors to their death. Many picturesque castles look down on the Rhine. The castles date from times when rulers who lived along the river levied tolls on passing ships. Today, ships sail free of charge. The river suffered serious pollution from spilled chemicals in 1986.

ALSO READ: GERMANY, POLLUTION.

RHINOCEROS   The rhinoceros is a large, heavy mammal with a thick, loose skin. Rhinoceroses have long bodies and heads but rather short legs. They weigh from 2,000 to 8,000 pounds (900 to 3,600 kg) and have one or two horns above the snout. The two African species have two horns. Three species—two with one horn and one with two horns—live in parts of Asia. These horns, made up of hairs stuck solidly together, can be very dangerous. But the rhinoceros's primary method of attack is charging. In spite of its size, the rhinoceros can charge rapidly when it senses danger. This animal is usually peaceful, however. Its eyesight is poor but its hearing and sense of smell are good.

Rhinoceroses are *herbivorous*—they eat grass and other plants. Rhinoceroses spend some of their time in water. They also wallow in the mud to get rid of insect parasites in their skin. A rhinoceros is most active when the weather is cool—in the morning and at night. It spends most of the day resting in the shade. It lives in grassy, marshy areas or in jungles. The rhinoceros usually lives alone, except during the breeding season. The female gives birth to one calf, which she nurses for about two years.

ALSO READ: HOOFED ANIMALS, HORNS AND ANTLERS, MAMMAL.

RHODE ISLAND

RHODE ISLAND Which state has the longest name? The state with the smallest area. Its full name is The State of Rhode Island and Providence Plantations. Rhode Island is a New England state bordered on the west by Connecticut and on the north and east by Massachusetts. The Atlantic Ocean is to the south.

One story about Rhode Island's name begins in the Mediterranean Sea. The Greek island of Rhodes lies near the coast of Turkey. In 1524, an Italian sea captain, Giovanni da Verrazano, was exploring the eastern coast of North America. He came to Block Island, off the mainland of present-day Rhode Island. This island, he reported, is "about the bigness of the Island of the Rhodes." Block Island is actually much smaller than Rhodes.

The English colonists who came later thought that Verrazano was describing another island. They thought it was the large island that the Indians called Aquidneck, which lies at the mouth of Narragansett Bay. The colonists renamed the island Rhode Island.

Settlements on the mainland were called the Providence Plantations. Eventually, the mainland and island settlements were made one colony, which was named Rhode Island and Providence Plantations. When the colony became a state in 1776, it kept its long name. But people have always used the short form.

The Land and Climate Rhode Island is only about 50 miles (80 km) long at its greatest length. Its greatest width is less than 50 miles (80 km). Of its total area, 165 square miles (427 sq. km) are water. The land area is 1,214 square miles (3,144 sq. km). With a population of about 968,000, Rhode Island has more people per square mile than any other state, except New Jersey.

Most of the water area is in Narragansett Bay. Two of the bay's arms are called the Providence River and the Sakonnet River. Rhode Island has 36 islands, most of which lie in the bay. Ten miles (16 km) out to sea is Block Island, named for Adriaen Block, a Dutch navigator. Its Great Salt Pond was turned into a harbor in 1900. A channel was dug to connect it to the ocean.

The rivers of the state are rather small, but they are useful. Their falls provide waterpower. The largest lake in the state is Scituate Reservoir, which was created by a dam across the Pawtuxet River. The lake supplies water to the city of Providence. Much of Rhode Island is made up of low, rounded hills.

On the whole, Rhode Island has a milder climate than the part of New England north of it. Rhode Island's precipitation is about right for farming. However, hurricanes have caused flooding and other damage in low-lying areas.

History When the first Europeans came to this region, five Indian tribes lived here. The most important were the Narraganset and Wampanoag.

Rhode Island was settled chiefly by English colonists from Massachusetts. The Puritans in Massachusetts

▲ *Two black rhinos in a game park in Tanzania.*

The longest horn on a white rhinoceros measured over 5 feet (158 cm). It is thought that explorers' reports of beasts like this led to the myth of the unicorn.

▲ *The dunes on Aquidneck Island, Rhode Island, are a pleasant place for a leisurely stroll.*

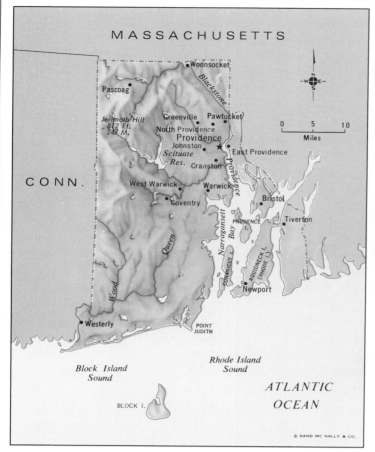

MASSACHUSETTS

Woonsocket

Pascoag

Jerimoth Hill
812 Ft.
247 M.

Greenville · Pawtucket
North Providence
Providence
Johnston
Scituate Res.
East Providence
Cranston

CONN.

West Warwick
Warwick

Coventry

Bristol

Tiverton

Narragansett Bay

PRUDENCE I.

CONANICUT I.

AQUIDNECK I. (RHODE I.)

Queen

Wood

Newport

Westerly

POINT JUDITH

Block Island Sound

Rhode Island Sound

ATLANTIC OCEAN

BLOCK I.

© RAND MC NALLY & CO.

0   5   10
Miles

▲ *A view over the spires of Providence, the capital and largest city in Rhode Island.*

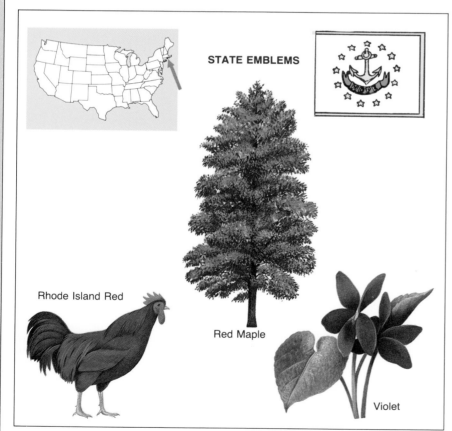

STATE EMBLEMS

HOPE

Rhode Island Red

Red Maple

Violet

RHODE ISLAND

Capital and largest city
Providence
(154,000 people)

Area
1,214 square miles (3,114 sq. km)
Rank: 50th

Population
993,000 people
Rank: 42nd

Statehood
May 29, 1790
(Last of the original 13 states to ratify the Constitution)

Principal rivers
Blackstone River
Pawtuxet River

Highest point
Jerimoth Hill
812 feet (247 m)
near the Connecticut boundary

Motto: "Hope"

Song: "Rhode Island"

Famous people
Ambrose Burnside, George M. Cohan, Nathanael Greene, Christopher and Oliver La Farge, Matthew C. and Oliver Perry, Gilbert Stuart

were hard on people who disagreed with them in matters of religion. In 1635, they told one such person, Roger Williams, to leave their colony. He bought land from the Narraganset Indians in what is now the state of Rhode Island. Williams named his settlement Providence; God's providence, or guidance, he said, had brought him there in his distress. The settlement is now the county and city of Providence.

Other people driven out of Massachusetts followed Roger Williams's example. They founded the towns of Portsmouth and Newport in 1638 and 1639. A fourth settlement, Warwick, was started south of Providence.

By 1654, all these settlements were one colony. A paper signed by King Charles II in 1663 stated, among other things, that people in the colony could worship as they pleased.

Like the rest of New England, the colony suffered from war. Rhode Islanders fought the French more than once. They fought Indians, too. The Indian war of 1675–1676 (called King Philip's War) started when settlers moved onto land held by the Wampanoags. The powerful Narragansets soon joined the Wampanoags. Towns in Massachusetts and Rhode Island were destroyed.

Rhode Islanders needed money to buy manufactured goods from Britain. They earned it by trade—buying and selling. Rhode Island, like Massachusetts, took part in a three-cornered trade. Rum made in Rhode Island was carried to Africa and exchanged for slaves. The slaves were taken to the sugar islands of the West Indies, where they were sold for molasses made from sugar. The molasses was brought back to Rhode Island for making rum. Every step in this trade earned a profit.

Newport was an important naval base during the American Revolution. Nathanael Greene, who was born in Rhode Island, was a leading American general in the revolution.

▲ *Newport Bridge connects the fashionable sailing and jazz-festival city of Newport, on Aquidneck Island, with the Rhode Island mainland.*

Industrial growth began in Rhode Island in the late 1700's. In 1790, an English industrialist, Samuel Slater, built the first successful spinning mill in the United States on the Blackstone River in present-day Pawtucket. (The restored mill still stands.) This mill spun cotton into yarn for weaving cloth. Other factories soon followed. People came to Rhode Island from Ireland, Italy, and eastern Europe to work in the factories. French Canadians also came.

Rhode Islanders at Work In the 1900's, southern textile mills took much business from those of New England. But some textiles are still manufactured in Rhode Island, along with jewelry, silverware, metal products, electronic equipment, and machine tools. Manufacturing is the state's main business. Most of the factories are grouped in the region around Providence. The area stretches from Pawtucket in the north to Warwick in the south. Providence is the state's capital and the second largest New England city.

Most Rhode Islanders live in towns and cities. But this little state, in spite of its large population, has room for farms. Dairy herds supply milk to cities. Some farmers keep poultry. Chickens called *Rhode Island Reds* are a favorite breed. The crop that earns

In Newport, Rhode Island, tourists can visit the oldest Quaker meetinghouse in America, the Friends Meeting House, built in 1699, and the oldest synagogue, the Touro Synagogue, built in 1763.

▲ *Cecil Rhodes, British colonial statesman.*

▲ *Colombian Indians pound rice into flour in a way unchanged for centuries.*

the most profit for farmers is potatoes. Apples, peaches, oats, and hay are also important crops. Perch, haddock, and other fish are caught in Rhode Island waters.

The first center of learning founded in Rhode Island was Rhode Island College, started in 1764. It is now Brown University.

Every summer, tourists come to Rhode Island to sail or go deep-sea fishing in the coastal waters. Yachts from other countries have met the best yachts from the United States in the America's Cup races off Newport. Visitors see the impressive Newport houses built by U.S. industrial magnates of the 1900's. A mysterious round tower known as the Old Stone Mill in Newport was probably built by early colonists as part of a grain mill. But Henry Wadsworth Longfellow was one of the people who thought that Vikings had built it. The tower is mentioned in his poem "The Skeleton in Armor." The U.S. Navy has a large base in Newport.

ALSO READ: MANUFACTURING; MASSACHUSETTS; VERRAZANO, GIOVANNI DA; VIKINGS; WILLIAMS, ROGER.

RHODES, CECIL (1853–1902) Cecil John Rhodes was a British administrator and businessman in South Africa. He helped to extend British control over that region.

Rhodes was born in Hertfordshire, England, and was educated at Oxford University. He spent his college vacations working at the diamond mines in Kimberly, South Africa. He later gained control over all the South African diamond mines and founded the DeBeers Consolidated Mines Company.

Rhodes's greatest ambition was to increase the power of the British Empire. He persuaded the British to take over Bechuanaland (now Botswana). The British South Africa Company,

which Rhodes had founded, opened new mines in the present-day regions of Zambia and Zimbabwe (known as Rhodesia in honor of Rhodes until 1979). These regions later became part of the British Empire.

Rhodes served as prime minister of the Cape Colony in South Africa from 1890 to 1896. He was forced to resign after a disastrous attempt to take over the Transvaal, an area already colonized by the Dutch.

Rhodes left a large sum of money in his will to be used as scholarships to Oxford University. The Rhodes Scholarships are awarded each year to students from several nations, including the United States.

ALSO READ: BOER WAR, DIAMOND, SOUTH AFRICA, ZIMBABWE.

RHYME see POETRY.

RHYTHM see DANCE, MUSIC, AND POETRY.

RICE Rice is one of the most important of all foods. It is the main food of millions of Asians. Rice is also eaten by other people in almost every country in the world.

Rice is a member of the family of cereal grasses, such as wheat, oats, and rye. There are many kinds of rice, but the kind most important for food has the name of *Oryza sativa*. It was developed from Asian wild rice.

People in Asia first sow rice seed in muddy, flooded fields. When the seedlings are a month to six weeks old, they are dug up and transplanted in even rows in *paddies*. Paddies are plowed fields covered with 3 or 4 inches (8 to 10 cm) of fresh water. The plants are pushed into the mud under the water and continue to grow in the paddies until they are harvested. The flooded fields are drained before the harvest.

Planting and harvesting of rice is done by hand in the Orient because many farmers there cannot afford to buy farm machinery. In other rice-growing areas, such as California, rice is planted by scattering seed from an airplane over a flooded field. The rice crop is harvested by machinery.

When ready for harvesting, the white rice grains have a coating of bran and are covered by a brown husk. The brown husk contains vitamins and minerals, but millions of people prefer the white grain, with the husks removed. This is called polished rice. In Asia, people who eat white rice, and almost nothing else, often suffer from *beriberi*. Beriberi is a disease that makes people unable to move their arms and legs. It comes from a shortage of the B-complex vitamins that are found in unpolished rice. Modern science has taught people that it is better to eat brown rice instead of white rice because the brown rice contains the B-vitamins. As a result, the use of brown rice is increasing.

More than 90 percent of the world's rice is produced in Asiatic countries. Other main rice-growing countries are the United States, Spain, Brazil, Egypt, and Italy.

ALSO READ: AGRICULTURE, ASIA, BUFFALO, FARM MACHINERY, FOOD, GRAIN, NUTRITION, VITAMINS AND MINERALS.

RICHARD, KINGS OF ENGLAND Richard is the name of three kings of England.

Richard I (1157–1199) was the son of Henry II of England and Eleanor of Aquitaine. Richard became king when his father died in 1189. Richard I neglected his country and spent much of his reign fighting wars abroad. He was given the nickname the "Lion-Hearted" because of his bravery in battle.

As soon as Richard was crowned, he gathered together an army and went on a *crusade* (holy war) to the Holy Land to free Jerusalem from the Muslims. The French king, Philip Augustus, also gathered an army and joined the crusade. The crusade ended in a truce, but Philip had begun to plot against Richard.

On the return journey, Richard was captured by the duke of Austria, a friend of Philip Augustus. Richard was held prisoner for three years until he was ransomed. When Richard finally returned to England, he started a war with Philip Augustus and was killed in battle.

Richard II (1367–1400) became king when he was only ten years old. The kingdom was ruled by Richard's uncle, John of Gaunt, until the king grew up. Because Richard was so young, the nobles of England thought they had a chance to gain more power for themselves. They began to fight among themselves and against the king. When Richard grew up, he managed to win control of his kingdom. He put to death many of the

▲ *Rice is a cereal grass that grows in warm, wet places. Because rice needs a lot of water, it is planted in flooded fields.*

▲ *A monument to Richard the Lion-Hearted stands in London, England.*

◀ *This painting of Richard II is the earliest contemporary (painted in his own lifetime) portrait of an English king to survive.*

▲ *Richard III of England.*

▲ *James Whitcomb Riley, the "Hoosier Poet."*

rebellious nobles. But his enemies finally forced him to give up his throne. Richard's cousin, Henry of Lancaster, was then crowned King Henry IV.

Richard III (1452–1485) is said to have gained his throne by murder and treachery. Richard was the brother of King Edward IV. Edward had two young sons. When King Edward died in 1483, his elder son, who was 12 years old, was crowned King Edward V. Richard was named Edward's protector.

Richard had himself declared king. Richard's enemies, led by Henry Tudor, revolted against him. Richard was killed at the Battle of Bosworth Field. Henry Tudor was then crowned King Henry VII. This was the end of the Wars of the Roses. Richard was accused of murdering his two young nephews. Richard's guilt is questioned by many historians. There is no proof that Richard murdered the young princes.

ALSO READ: CRUSADES; EDWARD, KINGS OF ENGLAND; ELEANOR OF AQUITAINE; ENGLISH HISTORY; HENRY, KINGS OF ENGLAND; JOHN, KING OF ENGLAND; WARS OF THE ROSES.

RIDING see HORSEBACK RIDING.

RIDDLE A riddle is a puzzling question that requires some clever thinking to answer correctly. It may be a problem with a hidden solution to be discovered or guessed. Riddles have been popular since ancient times.

Early people took their riddles seriously and often felt humiliated if they couldn't solve them. According to legend, the Greek poet Homer is said to have died of shame because he couldn't find the answer to a riddle. Prophets, oracles, poets, and minstrels presented many riddles for ordinary people to work out.

In Greek mythology, a famous riddle was asked by the Sphinx, a winged monster with a lion's body and a woman's head. "What walks on four legs in the morning, two at noon, and three at night?" The Sphinx destroyed all those who passed by if they were unable to give the correct answer. Oedipus, a Greek hero, solved the riddle. A person crawls on all fours when a baby, walks on two legs as an adult, and walks with a cane in old age. The Sphinx was so upset that she killed herself.

Riddles were very common in Europe during the Middle Ages. Here is an old English riddle. "When is a door not a door?" The answer, "When it is ajar." This kind of riddle is also called a *pun*. A pun is a play on words, using a word or words to suggest different meanings. A riddle whose answer is a pun is called a *conundrum*. Most modern riddles are conundrums. Two current, well-known riddles or conundrums are: "What has four wheels and flies?" A garbage truck. "What is black and white and read all over?" A newspaper.

A riddle with pictures is called a *rebus*. The pictures represent words, syllables, or sounds. A rebus may contain numbers, symbols, and letters, as well as drawings and words. One of the most familiar rebuses is the debtor's IOU for "I owe you."

ALSO READ: SPHINX, WORD GAMES.

RIFLE see GUNS AND RIFLES.

RILEY, JAMES WHITCOMB (1849–1916) James Whitcomb Riley was an American poet. He became known for his poetry written in the Indiana country dialect (type of speech). He wrote many poems for and about children. *Little Orphant Annie* is one of Riley's best-known poems. Little Orphant Annie was a young servant who told ghost stories at night. Each story ended with the frightening statement,

> An' the Gobble-uns'll git you
> Ef you don't watch out!

Riley, born in Greenfield, Indiana, is often called the "Hoosier Poet." (People who live in Indiana are called Hoosiers.) Riley left school at 16 and became a traveling sign painter. Later, he went to work for newspapers in Greenfield and Indianapolis. Riley wrote poems for the *Indianapolis Journal*, and they soon became very popular. In 1883, his first book of poetry, *The Old Swimmin' Hole and 'Leven More Poems*, was published. Other books of Riley's poems include *Afterwhiles, Rhymes of Childhood, Poems Here at Home*, and *The Book of Joyous Children*. Riley's work shows an understanding of and fondness for the people of Indiana.

ALSO READ: INDIANA, POETRY.

RIMSKY-KORSAKOV, NICOLAI (1844–1908) One of the most important musical figures in the 1800's was the Russian composer, Nicolai Rimsky-Korsakov. He is probably best remembered for his romantic orchestral work, *Scheherezade*. Among Rimsky-Korsakov's famous pieces are "The Flight of the Bumblebee" from the opera *Tsar Saltan*, and "Song of India" from the opera *Sadko*.

Rimsky-Korsakov was born in Tikhvin in northwestern Russia. At an early age, he displayed extraordinary musical talent. His parents, however, sent him to the naval academy at St. Petersburg (now Leningrad). During a three-year naval cruise, Rimsky-Korsakov wrote his first symphony. In 1871, he left the navy and began composing music. He became part of "The Russian Five," consisting of Mili Balakirev, César Cui, Modest Moussorgsky, Aleksandr Borodin, and himself. This group wrote music in a distinctively Russian style. Rimsky-Korsakov's music contains many Russian folk themes.

Rimsky-Korsakov was a professor of musical composition at the St. Petersburg Conservatory for more than 35 years. He composed choral works, piano pieces, and overtures, as well as symphonies and operas. Several of his students, including Sergei Prokofiev and Igor Stravinsky, later became famous as composers and conductors.

ALSO READ: MUSIC; OPERA; ORCHESTRAS AND BANDS; PROKOFIEV, SERGEI; STRAVINSKY, IGOR.

▲ *Nicolai Rimsky-Korsakov, Russian composer.*

RIO DE JANEIRO Rio de Janeiro is the greatest port of Brazil and for a long time was the capital of that country. Few cities have so beautiful a setting as Rio de Janeiro. Its huge bay is lined with fine sand beaches such as the Copacabana. Mountain peaks form a backdrop. One peak, called Sugar Loaf, 1,325 feet (404 m) high, dominates the entrance to the bay. Another peak, *Corcovado* ("the Hunchback"), reaches 2,300 feet (700 m) and is crowned by a giant statue of Christ the Redeemer.

The people of Rio, often called *Cariocans*, come from every country in the world. Only one person in eight is of pure Portuguese descent. A cheerful and lively people, their love of life

▼ *Shacks and skyscrapers show poverty and wealth side by side in Rio de Janeiro.*

▲ *In Big Bend National Park, the Rio Grande flows through this high, rocky canyon.*

▲ *The Yellowstone River plunges over a series of spectacular waterfalls into the breathtaking Grand Canyon of the Yellowstone.*

is best shown in the Mardi Gras Carnival the city celebrates every year before Lent. Cariocans love sport, and the largest football (soccer) stadium in the world is in Rio.

Rio is a busy marketing city for such important Brazilian products as coffee, cotton, and diamonds. The city has factories for clothing, food, metals, and chemicals. Rio's population is about five million people, which now ranks it second in Brazil to São Paulo.

Portuguese explorers visited the area about 1502. The French established a colony there in 1555, but they were soon driven out by the Portuguese. The traditional date of Rio's founding by the Portuguese is 1565. In the 1800's, when Brazil was a Portuguese colony, the French general Napoleon occupied Portugal. The Portuguese royal family fled from Lisbon in Portugal to Rio de Janeiro and soon made it into a splendid city. Rio was made the capital of independent Brazil in 1822 and remained so until 1960, when Brasília became the capital.

ALSO READ: BRAZIL, SÃO PAULO.

RIO GRANDE The Rio Grande is the fifth longest river in North America. It forms the border between the United States and Mexico for almost 1,300 miles (2,100 km). The river flows a distance of more than 1,800 miles (2,900 km) from its source in the San Juan Mountains of southwestern Colorado. The Rio Grande grows wider as it flows through New Mexico. It meets Mexico at El Paso, Texas, and then flows southeastward forming the boundary. The Rio Grande often floods when rain comes in sudden cloudbursts. It empties into the Gulf of Mexico near Brownsville, Texas, and Matamoros, Mexico. (See the map with the article on the UNITED STATES OF AMERICA.)

Americans call this river the Rio Grande, which means "big river" in Spanish. Mexicans call it Rio Bravo, "mighty river." Cars and people can easily cross the river on several toll bridges between the United States and Mexico. An agreement between the two countries forbids all navigation on the river.

Farmers of both nations use Rio Grande water to irrigate their fields. Large dams, such as the Amistad Dam and Falcon Dam, have been constructed jointly by the United States and Mexico. The dams control floods and provide water for irrigation. Cotton, vegetables, and citrus fruits bloom in the lower Rio Grande Valley because of the irrigation water.

■ **LEARN BY DOING**

Once when the Rio Grande changed its course, a tract of land near El Paso that had been Mexican shifted to the U.S. side. The United States, through President Lyndon Johnson, returned the land to Mexico in 1964. Can you think of other problems that might come up from having a river as a boundary? Would you put the exact line right down the middle of the stream? What agreements would be needed before dams and bridges could be built? ■

ALSO READ: MEXICAN WAR, MEXICO, RIVER, TEXAS.

RIVER Most rivers begin life as streams of water in the mountains. The small streams flow downhill and join other streams to form a river that goes on to the sea or a lake. Melting snow and rain make the river larger. A stream that flows into a larger stream is called a *tributary*.

■ **LEARN BY DOING**

A river with all its tributaries is called a *river system*. Look at a map of the United States. Can you find the main tributaries of the big Mississippi River? The largest of these tributaries

▲ *The waters of Bear River in Petoskey, Michigan. Rivers can be very rough when they flow over rocks or swell from heavy winter snowfalls.*

THE LONGEST RIVERS IN THE WORLD

River	Approximate length (miles/kilometers)	Location
Nile	4,160/6,695	Africa
Amazon	3,900/6,276	South America
Mississippi-Missouri System	3,860/6,212	North America
Yangtze	3,600/5,793	Asia
Ob-Irtysh System	3,010/4,844	Asia
Yellow (Hwang Ho)	3,010/4,844	Asia
Congo	2,900/4,667	Africa
Parana	2,700/4,345	South America
Lena	2,650/4,265	Asia
Mackenzie River	2,635/4,241	North America
Niger	2,600/4,184	Africa
Yenisei	2,570/4,136	Asia
Mekong	2,500/4,023	Asia
Mississippi	2,350/3,782	North America
Missouri	2,315/3,726	North America
Murray-Darling System	2,310/3,717	Australia

are the Missouri River, Arkansas River, and Ohio River. A *drainage basin* is the area from which tributaries collect rainwater.

Now move your finger onto the Mississippi River itself. Trace "Old Man River" from its *source* in Minnesota to its *delta* in Louisiana. Notice how it flows in gentle curves. The Mississippi flows through a flat plain and has no need to twist to avoid obstacles. ■

Did you know a river can be called young or old? A young river gathers water into a swift-running current. The water leaps down waterfalls and rapids on its way. The current breaks particles of soil and rock from the banks and carries them downstream. The particles "sandpaper" the sides and bed, or bottom, of the river and cut it deeper. This cutting action is called *erosion*. Such erosion may cut a canyon or gorge. The Grand Canyon of the Colorado River is the largest river canyon in the world.

As the river reaches "middle age," it has worn its valley down to a more gradual slope. The river has widened. The current moves more slowly. There is less erosion. The river forms broad loops, called *meanders*.

When the river reaches "old age,"

▶ *Landscape features formed by a river:*
(1) V-shaped valley
(2) Waterfall
(3) Gorge
(4) Meander
(5) Oxbow lake
(6) Flood plain
(7) Delta

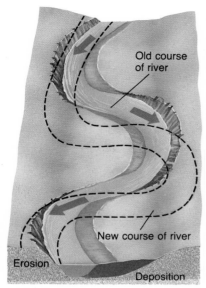

▲ *A meandering river changes its shape. River currents hit the outside curve of a meander, where erosion occurs. On the inside of the bend, mud and sand are deposited. The two act together and change the shape of the meander.*

▲ *Jackie Robinson leaps nimbly over a player sliding into second base.*

its current moves even more slowly. Particles of rock are deposited on the riverbed, making it shallower, and over the river's wide valley floor (*floodplain*) during times of flooding. The river meanders across the floodplain until it reaches the sea. Most rivers become very wide at their mouths, and some form deltas of deposited sediment.

The people who first inhabited North America, like people everywhere, usually settled along rivers. The river provided drinking, cooking, and washing water. The people could catch fish. The river provided a natural highway—all you had to do was build a boat or barge. When people began to raise crops, river valleys provided fertile soil.

Today, farmers still cultivate river valleys. But people have learned to use river water before it drains into the sea. Huge dams, which halt the flow of the water, can turn turbines and generate electricity. Reservoirs collect river water and pipe it to cities and parched fields. Rivers that once carried Indian canoes now carry huge ships.

ALSO READ: DAM, FLOOD, IRRIGATION, WATERFALL, WATER SUPPLY.

ROADS   see STREETS AND ROADS.

ROBIN HOOD   According to legend, the outlaw and hero, Robin Hood, came from a noble family and lived in England during the 1100's. When still a boy, he killed a man accidentally and was forced to flee into Sherwood Forest. He dressed in dark green and became highly skilled with a bow and arrow. Robin led a loyal band of "merry men," including Friar Tuck, Little John, Will Scarlet, and Alan-a-Dale. Maid Marian, Robin Hood's lady love, shared many of his adventures.

Robin first met Little John one day

on a bridge. Neither would let the other pass. Little John, who was 7 feet (2 m) tall and very strong, toppled Robin Hood into the stream. Robin immediately asked Little John to join his men.

Robin delighted in robbing the rich and giving their money to the poor. The Sheriff of Nottingham tried unsuccessfully again and again to capture Robin. Robin died when a treacherous cousin, pretending to help him, actually caused him to bleed to death. Some people think that Robin Hood was the Earl of Huntingdon, a Saxon who lost his lands to the invading Normans.

ROBINSON, JACKIE (1919–1972) Jackie Robinson was the first black player in American major-league baseball. He was an outstanding natural athlete in every sport he played.

Jack Roosevelt Robinson was born on a poor sharecropper's farm in Cairo, Georgia. His father died when Jackie was five years old, and his family moved to Pasadena, California, where he grew up. While he was in high school, Jackie worked at part-time jobs. But he also managed to play on his school's football, basketball, baseball, and track teams. He starred in football and baseball at the University of California at Los Angeles. He was also the National Collegiate broad jumping champion in 1940.

Robinson became a lieutenant in the U.S. Army in World War II. He signed up to play baseball for the Brooklyn Dodgers after the war. Robinson's career with the Dodgers lasted from 1947 until 1956. During that time, the Dodgers won six National League pennants and one World Series.

Robinson's lifetime batting average was .311. In 1962, he became the first black player elected to the Baseball Hall of Fame.

ALSO READ: BASEBALL.

ROBOT A robot is a machine that acts like a person or does the work of a person. The word "robot" comes from the Czech word for work—*robota*—and was first used in a play about robots written by the Czech writer, Karel Capek, in the 1920's. At that time, a robot was only an idea, but recently simple robots have become a reality.

If a robot is going to act like a person, it cannot simply *act*—it must also *react*. It must be able to change what it is doing as the situation changes. If you are riding your bicycle toward an intersection and you see a car coming, you know to stop. You react to the car by changing what you are doing. The bicycle does not react. If it weren't for you, it would roll into the intersection.

In order to react, the robot must be able to pick up information from outside itself and compare this information with what it already "knows" and what it "wants" to do. From this comparison, it must decide what to do next. All of this must be done in an instant.

Robots should not be confused with sophisticated remote control devices. These perform tasks such as handling radioactive materials or

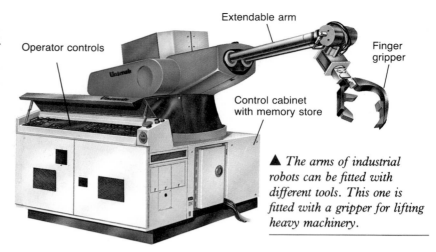

▲ The arms of industrial robots can be fitted with different tools. This one is fitted with a gripper for lifting heavy machinery.

working with bomb disposal teams. But they are not really robots at all because they do not carry out their tasks automatically. They are operator-controlled, a useful extension of their human masters.

The electronic computer has made it possible for a robot to sort out information and react quickly. The perfect robot, one that could do everything a person can do, has not yet been made. Most robots can do certain limited things and react to certain kinds of changes. An automatic pilot in an airplane "reads" the airplane's instruments and steers the plane the way a human pilot would. But it cannot get out of the plane and drive a car home. Robotlike machines can

▼ This unmanned NASA tele-operator vehicle is a robot designed to perform work on the surface of distant planets, where no human could survive.

▼ A robot drills an automobile part in a specially designed jig at this modern automobile assembly plant.

▲ *A tough granite outcrop stands where the softer rock around it has been eroded away.*

be "trained" to do jobs in a factory. They work at welding, paint spraying, loading and unloading, or feeding parts into machines. Certain robots can be used as substitutes for human beings in scientific research. Few of these robots look like people. One robot that does look like a person was built to test space suits for the astronauts. This robot can bend like a human being can, shrug its shoulders, and even dance. Recently, a robot has been built that keeps itself "alive." This robot "knows" it is not safe to walk downstairs, because it might fall. Whenever its batteries get low, the robot carefully plugs itself into an electrical outlet and systematically recharges its own power packs.

ALSO READ: COMPUTER.

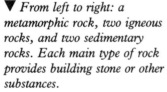

▼ *From left to right: a metamorphic rock, two igneous rocks, and two sedimentary rocks. Each main type of rock provides building stone or other substances.*

ROCK The whole Earth is surrounded by a crust of rock from 15 to 40 miles (24 to 64 km) thick. Most of the crust is covered by water and soil, but in many places the rocky crust is bare.

Rock is a solid material made up of minerals. The minerals vary and are not always combined in the same proportions. The rock called granite contains several minerals. The mineral called orthoclase may make up one-quarter to one-half of the granite. The mineral quartz may make up one-tenth to one-quarter. And the other minerals vary between one-fifth and one-quarter each. Pieces of granite with different proportions of each mineral may have different weights, colors, and textures.

Kinds of Rock There are three main kinds of rocks—*igneous, sedimentary*, and *metamorphic*.

IGNEOUS ROCKS. Igneous, or "firemade," rocks come from molten rock, called *magma*, that lies under the Earth's crust. From time to time, masses of magma push slowly upward through the crust. The rising magma cools and hardens. Millions of years later, the crust above the cooled magma may be worn away by *erosion*. Then, the mass of igneous rock is exposed to view.

Sometimes, the rising magma reaches cracks or weak places in the crust. It flows out upon the surface of the Earth through volcanoes or through long cracks, called *fissures*. Magma that reaches the Earth's surface is called *lava*. Parts of Oregon, Washington, and Idaho were formed by immense flows of lava. Granite and basalt are the two most common igneous rocks.

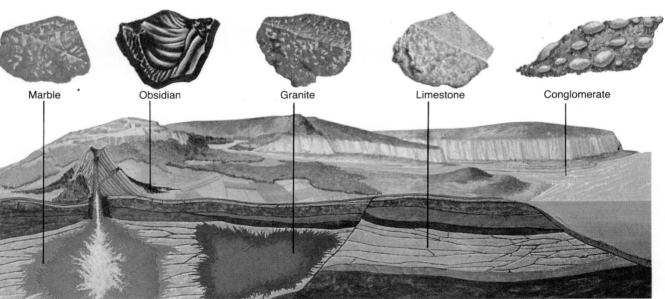

Marble   Obsidian   Granite   Limestone   Conglomerate

SEDIMENTARY ROCKS. The rocks on the Earth's surface are continually being broken up into small grains through the action of weather, running water, wind, glaciers, and gravity. Running water carries away most of the rock grains, called *sediment*. Mud, clay, and sand are kinds of sediment. The sediment piles up at the mouths of rivers or wherever the water slows down enough so that it can sink to the bottom.

When sediment is piled to great depths, the weight of the upper layers presses down on the lower layers with tremendous force. This squeezes water from between the grains. Sometimes the water contains dissolved minerals that act as cement. Eventually, all the water is squeezed out, and the grains are pressed together into a solid mass of rock—sedimentary rock.

Rock fragments are not the only source of sedimentary rock. Large areas of the Earth are covered with a rock called limestone. Coral animals, shellfish, and the tiny plants called *diatoms* take a mineral called *calcium carbonate* out of seawater. They use it to form their skeletons or shells. When they die, they sink to the bottom of the sea. In millions of years, their broken skeletons and shells pile up in layers thousands of feet thick. Pressure eventually changes these layers into limestone. Chalk is a kind of limestone. Limestone is also formed from calcium carbonate deposited by water.

METAMORPHIC ROCKS. When masses of magma push upward into the Earth's crust, sedimentary or igneous rocks nearby are heated and put under pressure. The heat and pressure may change these rocks to metamorphic, or "changed-form," rock. For example, limestone is changed to marble, and the rock called shale is changed to slate. Rock may also be metamorphosed (changed into a different form) because of shifts in the Earth's crust.

■ **LEARN BY DOING**

Being a "rock-hound," or collector of rocks, is fun and can teach you much about the Earth. It is easy to find rocks—even in a city. You can start by getting a book that will tell you how to find and identify interesting rocks. ■

ALSO READ: EARTH, EROSION, GEOLOGY, GRANITE, MINERAL, VOLCANO.

ROCKET You can make a very simple rocket out of a balloon. Just fill the balloon with air and let it go. The air rushes out of the mouth of the balloon, and the balloon flies across the room.

The balloon is a compressed-air rocket. When you blow into it, you force a large amount of air into a small space. The rubber of the balloon stretches from the air pressure. The air pushes in all directions equally and is contained by an equal force in all directions if the mouth of the balloon is closed (A). But both the air and the rubber of the balloon are elastic, and if the mouth of the balloon is open, the air under pressure rushes out of it (B). The rubber of the balloon begins to shrink to its normal size. The pressure of the air inside the balloon is now much greater in the direction opposite the mouth than that at the mouth. The balloon flies in the direction opposite the mouth. All rockets work on this principle. By allowing a

▲ *The Grand Canyon gives us a section through the Earth's history. Pre-Cambrian rocks at the bottom are overlaid with Cambrian, Carboniferous, and Permian rocks.*

▲ *The Chinese invented the first firework rocket, but they also fired rockets as weapons of war.*

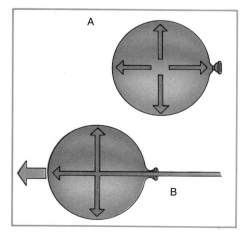

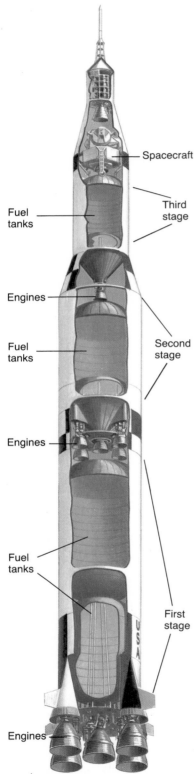

Spacecraft

Fuel tanks

Third stage

Engines

Fuel tanks

Second stage

Engines

Fuel tanks

First stage

Engines

USA

▲ *This rocket launched the Apollo spacecraft to the moon and weighed about 3,000 tons (3,048 metric tons) at lift-off. Over 2,000 tons (2,030 metric tons) of this was fuel for the first stage of the rocket.*

gas under pressure to escape from the end, they are driven in the direction opposite that end.

Compressed air is a kind of propellant—it moves a rocket—but it is not a powerful propellant. As in fireworks, rockets use a propellant that burns, giving off a hot gas that pushes the rocket at high speeds through the air.

The gas does not have to push *against* anything. This is one reason why a rocket can move through empty space. Another reason is that the rocket propellant carries its own oxygen. Burning is just a rapid kind of oxidation—the combining of oxygen and another substance. All burning requires oxygen. A jet engine gets its oxygen from the air, so a jet can only fly in air. A rocket carries its own oxygen, so it can fly in empty space. A complete rocket propellant includes a *fuel* that burns and an *oxidizer* that makes the fuel burn. Some fuels and oxidizers burn on contact. Others need a spark to set them off. Rockets can use solid or liquid propellants.

In a simple solid-propellant engine, the propellant is a solid cake, or *grain*, attached to the inner walls of a tubular casing. The grain contains both the oxidizer and the fuel. The casing serves as the container for the propellant and as the combustion chamber. An opening, often star-shaped, through the middle of the grain allows the grain to burn evenly outwards. A nozzle at the open end of the casing controls the flow of hot gases.

A liquid-fuel engine has a separate fuel and oxidizer. The propellants are held in tanks outside the combustion chamber and are fed into the chamber by pumps or by pressurized gas. In the chamber, the liquids change to vapor and are ignited. The flow of hot gases produced is controlled by a nozzle.

The liquid-fuel engine has several advantages over the solid fuel engine. Its performance is usually higher, as

measured by the velocity of the exhaust gases. The flow and burning of liquid fuel is easier to control, and a liquid-fuel engine can be turned off and on. Liquid-fuel engines are usually more powerful. The most powerful liquid-fuel rocket that has been publicized is the Soviet Energia. It is more powerful than the Saturn V, whose first-stage engines produce 7,570,000 pounds (3,435,000 kg) of thrust. Saturn V was used for the Apollo and Skylab programs. The most powerful solid-fuel rocket engines are the two boosters used on the Space Shuttle.

The multiple-stage rocket consists of several rocket engines set one on top of another. The booster, or first stage engine, is fired first. When the first stage has burned up its fuel, it drops away, and the second stage ignites. When the second stage has exhausted its fuel, the third stage ignites. Most multiple-stage rockets

▼ *The Space Shuttle blasts off with all the power of its main rocket engine and two booster rockets.*

ROCKETS USED IN THE MANNED SPACE PROGRAM OF THE UNITED STATES

Rocket	Height (ft./m)	Stages	Thrust (lb./kg)	Diameter (ft./m)	Fuel	Importance
Redstone	83/25.3	1	82,000/37,200	5.7/1.7	Aerozine 50, a liquid fuel	Sent America's first man into space (Alan Shepard) aboard Mercury spacecraft
Atlas (Series D)	67/20.4	1½	360,000/163,300	10/3	Kerosene and liquid oxygen	First launch vehicle in the free world to orbit a man (John Glenn). Also it was the first operational Intercontinental Ballistic Missile (ICBM).
Titan II	103/31.4	2	530,000/240,400	10/3	Nitrogen tetroxide and mixture of hydrazine and dimethyl hydrazine	Launched the Gemini spacecraft
Saturn V	364/111	3	(1) 7,570,000/3,400,000	(1) 33/10	Kerosene and liquid oxygen	Launched Apollo spacecraft to the moon
			(2) 1,000,000/453,600	(2) 33/10	Liquid hydrogen & liquid oxygen	
			(3) 200,000/90,700	(3) 21.7/6.6	Liquid oxygen & liquid hydrogen	

have three stages. The multiple staging allows the rockets to use a powerful booster to provide the initial launching thrust, without having to carry the weight of the booster throughout the flight.

The Chinese used rockets in warfare in the 1200's. For the next several hundred years, most rockets were designed as weapons. Then, in the late 1800's, a Russian scientist, Konstantin Tsiolkovsky, suggested that rockets could be used in space travel. He proposed the *multiple-stage*, or *step*, rocket. Most space flights today are multistage rockets.

Tsiolkovsky also proposed using liquid fuel for rockets. In 1926, Dr. Robert Goddard, an American scientist, built the first liquid-fuel rocket.

The 10-foot-long (3-m-long) rocket flew 184 feet (56 m) in about 2½ seconds on its maiden flight. This flight marked the beginning of modern rocketry. Most large rockets since then have used liquid fuel.

During World War II, the most important advances in rocketry were made in Germany. German V-2 rockets were fired across the English Channel, badly damaging London and killing many people.

Since the war, the most important research has been carried on in the United States and the Soviet Union. Both countries have built many rockets for space exploration and military use. In 1957, the first man-made satellite, the Soviet Sputnik I, was launched by rocket. Shortly after-

▼ *Large modern rockets are liquid-fueled. The fuel is stored in a tank inside the rocket. A second tank contains liquid oxygen. To fire the rocket, these two substances are brought together by means of various pumps and mixers. This happens at the tail end of the rocket and results in an intensely fierce burning or combustion.*

LIQUID PROPELLANT ROCKET

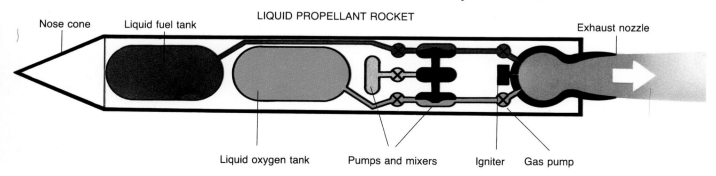

Nose cone Liquid fuel tank   Exhaust nozzle

Liquid oxygen tank   Pumps and mixers   Igniter   Gas pump

▲ *Knute Rockne, football coach.*

ward, the first American satellite, Explorer I, was launched by a Redstone rocket.

The Apollo space flights were powered by Saturn rockets. These multistage, liquid-fuel rockets were 364 feet (111 m) high and were powerful enough to carry over 50 tons (45 metric tons) to the moon. These were not the only rockets used on the Apollo flights. Smaller rockets were fired to change the direction of flight and to soften the spacecrafts' landings on the moon.

The Space Shuttle employs a combination of two separate solid-fuel boosters and a liquid-fuel engine in the shuttle to reach orbit. Both the boosters and the shuttle itself are designed to be used again. Only the tank for the liquid fuels is discarded. The Space Shuttle made its first flight in 1981.

ALSO READ: GODDARD, ROBERT H.; JET PROPULSION; PHYSICS; SPACE RESEARCH; SPACE TRAVEL.

ROCK MUSIC see POPULAR MUSIC.

ROCKNE, KNUTE (1888–1931) Knute Rockne was one of the greatest American Football coaches. He coached at Notre Dame University for 13 years. His teams won 105 games, lost only 12, and tied 5.

Rockne was born in Voss, Norway. He and his parents came to Chicago, Illinois, when Knute was five years old. He went to Notre Dame University, where he majored in chemistry. He played end and halfback for Notre Dame in 1912 and 1913. Although he was small compared to today's football players, Rockne was outstanding on the gridiron. The forward pass was a new play then, and Rockne and his teammates perfected it. As a result, Notre Dame stunned the football world by beating Army in 1913.

Rockne was made assistant coach at Notre Dame in 1914, and head coach in 1918. He drilled his players endlessly in football fundamentals—blocking and tackling. His teams were always among the best in the country. Everyone in the sports world was saddened when this great coach was killed in an airplane crash in Kansas in 1931.

ALSO READ: FOOTBALL.

ROCKY MOUNTAINS The Rocky Mountains extend through the western part of North America from Alaska all the way to Mexico. The "Rockies" provide magnificent scenery for those who live in or visit Montana, Idaho, Wyoming, Nevada, Utah, Colorado, Arizona, and New Mexico. Most of the highest mountain peaks in North America are in the Rockies. (See the map with the article on NORTH AMERICA.)

The Rocky Mountains were formed millions of years ago as volcanic action pushed the Earth's crust upward thousands of feet. Within this mountain system are many individual mountain ranges. Pacific Ocean winds drop their moisture when they reach the cool, high mountains, and most rainfall and snowfall occurs on the western side of the Rocky Moun-

The area covered by the Rocky Mountain States is more than a fourth of the entire United States. The states are Colorado, Idaho, Montana, Nevada, Utah, and Wyoming.

▼ *Cattle graze on the foothills of the Rockies. East of the mountains, prairie and forest stretch all the way to the Great Lakes.*

tains. High plateaus called "parks" lie between the ranges. Vegetation is heavier in the parks. The higher peaks stay snow-covered all year round. Low stretches of hot, dry desert are found in the southern Rockies.

The highest peak in the Rockies is Mount Elbert, 14,431 feet (4,399 m) high, in Colorado. The Continental Divide runs along the highest peaks of the Rockies and cuts through North America from north to south. Rivers in the United States west of the Divide flow toward the Pacific Ocean, and east of the Divide flow toward the Mississippi River.

Every year, many visitors go to see Yellowstone National Park or the Grand Canyon, which the Colorado River has cut through the Rockies. In Canada, Banff National Park and Jasper National Park present scenic snowcapped mountains and glaciers. Ski resorts are very popular.

Goats and bighorn sheep live high in the Rockies. Bears, deer, coyotes, mountain lions, and other animals live in the forests lower down.

When the pioneers reached the Rockies from the Great Plains, they were faced with mountains that seemed impossible to cross. But caravans on horseback and in wagons moved along the Oregon Trail through mountain passes to the Northwest. Stagecoaches later replaced the covered wagons. Trains replaced the stagecoaches.

Among the first white people to settle in the Rockies were prospectors searching for minerals. Today, mining is an important industry in the Rocky Mountain states. Rich veins of copper, lead, silver, gold, and zinc run through the mountains. There are also valuable deposits of oil, oil shale, natural gas, phosphate, and bituminous (soft) coal.

ALSO READ: CONTINENTAL DIVIDE, GRAND CANYON, MOUNTAIN, YELLOWSTONE PARK.

▲ Nobility and Virtue, *part of a ceiling fresco by the Italian painter, Giovanni Battista Tiepolo.*

ROCOCO ART In the 1700's in Europe, a style of art and architecture known as Rococo became popular. It spread all across Europe, including England. Rococo was a decorated, sentimental style. Rococo decor drew its inspiration from natural objects in which the lines move freely—flowers, seaweed, and above all, seashells.

The style had its beginnings in the churches and palaces of the south German provinces. The German princes wanted their territories to have beautiful churches and palaces of which they could be proud. The 1700's were a time of deep religious feeling. And Rococo in church architecture was graceful and enthusiastic of spirit. Church interiors were often white and gold. Two families, the Asams and the Zimmermanns created the German Baroque style, which soon became indistinguishable from Rococo.

Perhaps the foremost decorator of this age was the Venetian painter, Giovanni Battista Tiepolo. He painted frescoes on the ceilings of many churches and palaces of the 1700's. His fresco painting on this page is *Nobility and Virtue*. He painted it in the Rezzonico Palace in the city of Venice. See Nobility and Virtue flying on the wings of a huge bird, while cherubs dart happily through the clouds.

The age of Rococo, besides producing fancy decor, was a great age

▲ *Ceres (the Roman goddess of agriculture) by the French painter, Jean Antoine Watteau. National Gallery of Art, Washington, D.C., Samuel H. Kress Collection.*

▲ *This salon in a house in Paris, France, was decorated in the 1730's. The style is elaborate and ornate, but the designs are flowing and graceful.*

for the creation of music in the German and Austrian provinces. Johann Sebastian Bach, Domenico Scarlatti, and George Frederick Handel wrote their Baroque and Rococo music, whose trills and embellishments seem to fit in with the architecture of the time. Such music was often played in the salon of the castle of Sans Souci in Potsdam, the home of King Frederick the Great. A great patron of music, King Frederick was a musician himself and played the flute very well. He entertained the composer Bach here, too. The Rococo setting seems made for a small music group. The white walls are decorated with gold—the flowers, cherubs, and the ever-present shell design in various interpretations. Even the music stand has

the twisted, intricate lines of Rococo.

The great painter of the age of Rococo was Antoine Watteau. He was born in Belgium, settled in France, and died at the young age of 37. He caught the delicate shades of feeling of the age of Rococo. Like Tiepolo, he designed interior decorations for the castles of the nobility. His dreams and ideals and his fashion for dainty colors and delicate decoration expressed the feeling of Rococo. See the beauty of line in his oval painting on page 2113 of Ceres, the goddess of grain and summer's growing season. Watteau loved to draw and paint beautiful girls. His folds of drapery shimmer, and he is a master of detail. Ceres is carrying a scythe, as the goddess of grain. Watteau expresses the spirit of Rococo, a lovely goddess sitting on a cloud, happy and serene.

Rococo influenced every kind of art. Opera houses all over Europe and Latin America were Rococo in design. Even Rococo knife handles and teapots were popular. It became an elegant, international style, dedicated to happiness.

ALSO READ: BACH FAMILY; BAROQUE PERIOD; HAYDN, FRANZ JOSEPH; MOZART, WOLFGANG AMADEUS.

▼ *Detail of a sofa armrest showing a Merman, a mythical creature of the sea, half-man, half-fish, carved in the fancy Rococo style. Such ornate work was popular in the early 1700's.*